# TEACHER'S PET PUBLICATIONS

LITPLAN TEACHER PACK
for
The Adventures of Huckleberry Finn

based on the book by
Mark Twain

Written by
Mary B. Collins

© 1996 Teacher's Pet Publications
All Rights Reserved

This **LitPlan** for Mark Twain's
Adventures of Huckleberry Finn
has been brought to you by Teacher's Pet Publications, Inc.

Copyright Teacher's Pet Publications 1996
11504 Hammock Point
Berlin MD 21811

Only the student materials in this unit plan (such as worksheets,
study questions, and tests) may be reproduced multiple times
for use in the purchaser's classroom.

For any additional copyright questions,
contact Teacher's Pet Publications.

www.tpet.com

TABLE OF CONTENTS - *Huckleberry Finn*

Introduction	6
Unit Objectives	8
Reading Assignment Sheet	9
Unit Outline	10
Study Questions (Short Answer)	13
Quiz/Study Questions (Multiple Choice)	21
Pre-reading Vocabulary Worksheets	37
Lesson One (Introductory Lesson)	57
Nonfiction Assignment Sheet	66
Oral Reading Evaluation Form	68
Writing Assignment 1	60
Writing Assignment 2	77
Writing Assignment 3	86
Writing Evaluation Form	82
Vocabulary Review Activities	78
Extra Writing Assignments/Discussion ?	80
Unit Review Activities	88
Unit Tests	91
Unit Resource Materials	125
Vocabulary Resource Materials	141

A FEW NOTES ABOUT THE AUTHOR
MARK TWAIN

TWAIN, Mark (1835-1910). A onetime printer and Mississippi River boat pilot, Mark Twain became one of America's greatest authors. His *Tom Sawyer, Huckleberry Finn*, and *Life on the Mississippi* rank high on any list of great American books.

Mark Twain was born Samuel Langhorne Clemens on Nov. 30, 1835, in the small town of Florida, Mo. He was the fourth of five children. His father was a hard worker but a poor provider. The family moved to Hannibal, Mo., on the Mississippi, when young Clemens was 4 years old. It was in this river town that he grew up, and from it he gathered the material for his most famous stories. The character of Judge Carpenter is somewhat like his father; Aunt Polly, his mother; Sid Sawyer, his brother Henry; Huck Finn, a town boy named Tom Blankenship; and Tom Sawyer, a combination of several boys-including himself.

His father died when he was 12, and the boy was apprenticed to a printer. An apprentice works for someone in order to learn a trade. This was the first step toward his career as a writer. In 1857 he apprenticed himself to a riverboat pilot. He became a licensed pilot and spent two and a half years at his new trade. The river swarmed with traffic, and the pilot was the most important man aboard the boat. He wrote of these years in *Life on the Mississippi*.

The Civil War ended his career as a pilot. Clemens went west to Nevada and soon became a reporter on the Virginia City newspaper. Here he began using the pen name Mark Twain. It is an old river term meaning two fathoms, or 12 feet (4 meters), of water depth.

In 1864 he went to California. The next year he wrote his "Jumping Frog" story, which ran in many newspapers. He was sent to the Sandwich Islands (now Hawaii) as a roving reporter, and on his return he began lecturing. He was soon on a tour of the Mediterranean and the Holy Land. From this came *The Innocents Abroad*, which made him famous.

In 1870 he married Olivia Langdon, daughter of a wealthy businessman of Elmira, N.Y. Olivia modified Twain's exaggerations, sometimes weakening his writings, sometimes actually making them more readable. They had three daughters.

Twain began turning out a new book every few years. William Dean Howells, editor of the Atlantic Monthly and a highly respected novelist, became his close friend and literary adviser. Twain bought a publishing firm in Hartford, Conn. He earned much money writing, lecturing, and in his publishing house, but he spent it on high living and unsuccessful investments. He lost a fortune promoting a typesetting machine. By 1894 his publishing company had failed and he was bankrupt.

Twain set out on a world lecture tour to retrieve his fortune, and by 1898 his debts were paid. In his last years he traveled and spoke much but wrote comparatively little. He died on April 21, 1910.

Twain was more than a humorist. Behind his mask of humor lay a serious view of life. Tragedy had entered his own life in the poverty and early death of his father, the loss of a daughter, and his bankruptcy. His short story, "The Man That Corrupted Hadleyburg", published in 1900, which showed greed at work in a small town, is an indication of Twain's dark side.

The controversial *Huckleberry Finn*, which is periodically banned in schools or libraries because of alleged racial overtones, can be read by children, but it is not a child's book. It has elements of heartbreak and wisdom that can be appreciated best by adults. On the other hand, *Tom Sawyer* is primarily a juvenile book but one that can be read with pleasure by adults.

Twain's chief works are: *The Celebrated Jumping Frog of Calaveras County*, a collection published in 1867; *The Innocents Abroad* (1869); *Roughing It* (1872); *The Gilded Age*-with Charles Dudley Warner (1873); *The Adventures of Tom Sawyer* (1876); *A Tramp Abroad* (1880); *The Prince and the Pauper* (1882); *Life on the Mississippi* (1883); *The Adventures of Huckleberry Finn* (1884); *A Connecticut Yankee in King Arthur's Court* (1889); *The Tragedy of Pudd'nhead Wilson* (1894); and *Personal Recollections of Joan of Arc* (1896). Printed posthumously were: *The Mysterious Stranger* (1916); *Mark Twain's Notebook* (1935); and *Autobiography* (1959).

---- Courtesy of Compton's Learning Company

INTRODUCTION - *Huckleberry Finn*

This unit has been designed to develop students' reading, writing, thinking, and language skills through exercises and activities related to *Huckleberry Finn* by Mark Twain. It includes twenty-five lessons, supported by extra resource materials.

The **introductory lesson** introduces students to the idea of dialects through a game-type activity. Following the introductory activity, students are given a transition to explain how the activity relates to the book they are about to read. Following the transition, students are given the materials they will be using during the unit. At the end of the lesson, students begin the pre-reading work for the first reading assignment.

The **reading assignments** are approximately thirty pages each; some are a little shorter while others are a little longer. Students have approximately 15 minutes of pre-reading work to do prior to each reading assignment. This pre-reading work involves reviewing the study questions for the assignment and doing some vocabulary work for 8 to 10 vocabulary words they will encounter in their reading.

The **study guide questions** are fact-based questions; students can find the answers to these questions right in the text. These questions come in two formats: short answer or multiple choice. The best use of these materials is probably to use the short answer version of the questions as study guides for students (since answers will be more complete), and to use the multiple choice version for occasional quizzes. If your school has the appropriate equipment, it might be a good idea to make transparencies of your answer keys for the overhead projector.

The **vocabulary work** is intended to enrich students' vocabularies as well as to aid in the students' understanding of the book. Prior to each reading assignment, students will complete a two-part worksheet for approximately 8 to 10 vocabulary words in the upcoming reading assignment. Part I focuses on students' use of general knowledge and contextual clues by giving the sentence in which the word appears in the text. Students are then to write down what they think the words mean based on the words' usage. Part II nails down the definitions of the words by giving students dictionary definitions of the words and having students match the words to the correct definitions based on the words' contextual usage. Students should then have an understanding of the words when they meet them in the text.

After each reading assignment, students will go back and formulate answers for the study guide questions. Discussion of these questions serves as a **review** of the most important events and ideas presented in the reading assignments.

After students complete reading the work, there is a **vocabulary review** lesson which pulls together all of the fragmented vocabulary lists for the reading assignments and gives students a review of all of the words they have studied.

Following the vocabulary review, a lesson is devoted to the **extra discussion questions/writing assignments**. These questions focus on interpretation, critical analysis and personal response, employing a variety of thinking skills and adding to the students' understanding of the novel.

There is a **Group Theme Project** in this unit. Students are divided into groups, one group for each major theme in the novel. Each group then has a series of assignments to do, all of which lead up to a class-period-long multi-media presentation about that theme. The actual presentation will have three parts: the theme in the novel, the theme in real life today, and a conclusion in which the first two parts are linked together if possible.

There are three **writing assignments** in this unit, each with the purpose of informing, persuading, or having students express personal opinions. The first assignment is to inform: students write compositions about their themes in the novel, based on the research they have done so far. The second assignment is to express personal opinions: students review the personality traits of the characters, pick which character they think they personally are most like, and write a composition explaining how they are like that character. The third assignment is to persuade: students evaluate the group theme projects and decide which they think was the best presentation. They then write a composition persuading the teacher that that presentation was, in fact, the best one.

The **nonfiction reading assignment** is tied in with the Group Theme Project. Students must read nonfiction articles, books, etc. to gather information about their themes in our world today. The information gathered while doing this reading is then incorporated into the students' theme presentations.

The **review lesson** pulls together all of the aspects of the unit. The teacher is given four or five choices of activities or games to use which all serve the same basic function of reviewing all of the information presented in the unit.

The **unit test** comes in two formats: multiple choice or short answer. As a convenience, two different tests for each format have been included. There is also an advanced short answer unit test for advanced students.

There are additional **support materials** included with this unit. The **extra activities packet** includes suggestions for an in-class library, crossword and word search puzzles related to the novel, and extra vocabulary worksheets. There is a list of **bulletin board ideas** which gives the teacher suggestions for bulletin boards to go along with this unit. In addition, there is a list of **extra class activities** the teacher could choose from to enhance the unit or as a substitution for an exercise the teacher might feel is inappropriate for his/her class. **Answer keys** are located directly after the **reproducible student materials** throughout the unit. The student materials may be reproduced for use in the teacher's classroom without infringement of copyrights. No other portion of this unit may be reproduced without the written consent of Teacher's Pet Publications.

UNIT OBJECTIVES - *Huckleberry Finn*

1. Through reading Mark Twain's *Huckleberry Finn*, students will gain a better understanding of the themes of education, freedom/bondage, nature, religion, and superstition both in the novel and in our real world today.

2. Students will demonstrate their understanding of the text on four levels: factual, interpretive, critical and personal.

3. Students will define their own viewpoints for the aforementioned themes.

4. Students will be exposed to a different era of American life, showing many of today's conflicts are not new; they are rooted in our American past.

5. Students will read various American dialects which show the often forgotten or ignored differences between the spoken and written language.

6. Students will be given the opportunity to practice reading aloud and silently to improve their skills in each area.

7. Students will answer questions to demonstrate their knowledge and understanding of the main events and characters in *Huckleberry Finn* as they relate to the author's theme development.

8. Students will enrich their vocabularies and improve their understanding of the novel through the vocabulary lessons prepared for use in conjunction with the novel.

9. The writing assignments in this unit are geared to several purposes:
    a. To have students demonstrate their abilities to inform, to persuade, or to express their own personal ideas
        Note: Students will demonstrate ability to write effectively to <u>inform</u> by developing and organizing facts to convey information. Students will demonstrate the ability to write effectively to <u>persuade</u> by selecting and organizing relevant information, establishing an argumentative purpose, and by designing an appropriate strategy for an identified audience. Students will demonstrate the ability to write effectively to <u>express personal ideas</u> by selecting a form and its appropriate elements.
    b. To check the students' reading comprehension
    c. To make students think about the ideas presented by the novel
    d. To encourage logical thinking
    e. To provide an opportunity to practice good grammar and improve students' use of the English language.

READING ASSIGNMENT SHEET - *Huckleberry Finn*

Date Assigned	Chapters Assigned	Completion Date
	1-3	
	4-7	
	8-11	
	12-14	
	15-18	
	19-25	
	26-31	
	32-39	
	40-43	

UNIT OUTLINE - *Huckleberry Finn*

1 Introduction PV 1-3	2 Read 1-3	3 Study ?s 1-3 PVR 4-7	4 Study ?s 4-7 PVR 8-11	5 Study ?s 8-11 Usage Worksheet PVR 12-14
6 Group Theme Project	7 Study ?s 12-14 PVR 15-18	8 Study ?s 15-18 Grammar Worksheet PVR 19-25	9 Study ?s 19-25 PVR 26-31	10 Study ?s 26-31 Group Theme Project (Library)
11 PVR 32-39	12 Study ?s 32-39 PVR 40-43	13 Study ?s 40-43 Group Theme Project (Class)	14 Writing Assignment 2	15 Vocabulary
16 Discussion Questions	17 Group Theme Project	18 Freedom	19 Religion	20 Superstition
21 Education	22 Nature	23 Theme Summary Writing Assignment 3	24 Review	25 Test

Key: P = Preview Study Questions V = Vocabulary Work R = Read

STUDY GUIDE QUESTIONS

SHORT ANSWER STUDY GUIDE QUESTIONS - *Huckleberry Finn*

Chapters 1-3
1. Identify: Huck Finn, Tom Sawyer, Jim, Miss Watson and Widow Douglas.
2. Why doesn't Huck get along with Miss Watson and Widow Douglas?
3. What does Huck think about religion -- specifically the good place, the bad place and prayer?
4. Give at least two examples of superstition in this section of the novel.
5. Contrast Huck and Tom. What are their main differences?

Chapters 4-7
1. Why did Huck give his money to Judge Thatcher?
2. Describe Pap Finn. What kind of a person is he?
3. What is Huck's attitude towards his father?
4. Why does Pap yell at Huck for becoming civilized? Is he right?
5. What was Huck's plan of escape from his father?
6. How do you know that material things don't matter to Huck?

Chapters 8 - 11
1. What purpose(s) does Huck's death serve?
2. How does Huck meet Jim on Jackson's Island? Why is Jim there?
3. What is in the two story house that floats by?
4. Give three examples of Man vs. Society in this section.
5. How are the townspeople superstitious? Jim? Huck? Give examples.
6. Compare/contrast Huck & Jim.
7. Why does Huck dress as a girl to go ashore? Why does he go? What does he find out?
8. How do you know Huck and Jim are friends by the end of Chapter XI?

Chapters 12-14
1. Why do Huck and Jim begin their journey down the Mississippi?
2. Why do Huck and Jim board the Walter Scott?
3. Why does Huck want to save Jim Turner?
4. How does Huck send help to the Walter Scott?
5. What do we learn about Jim from his talking about "King Sollermun"?

Chapters 15-18
1. What trick does Huck play on Jim?
2. Why doesn't Huck turn in Jim?
3. Why don't the slave hunters get Jim?
4. Explain the differences between Huck and the hunters.
5. What is the bad luck in Chapter 16?
6. How does Huck get to the Grangerfords?
7. Why did Twain include this adventure with the Grangerfords?

Huckleberry Finn Short Answer Study Guide Page 2

Chapters 19-25
1. How did Jim and Huck meet the king and duke?
2. Does Huck believe their story?
3. Give two examples of the "cleverness" of the king and duke.
4. Why did the people return to the show?
5. What's the point of the incident of the shooting of Boggs?
6. Why do we hear about Jim's daughter "'Lizabeth"?
7. Where did the king and duke get their plan about being the Wilks brothers?

Chapters 26-31
1. How do the king and duke get the money?
2. Why does Huck steal the money from the mattress?
3. Why doesn't Huck's conscience bother him when he lies so much?
4. What things give away the king and duke?
5. Why is Huck upset when Jim is sold?
6. Why it is important that Huck says, "All right, then, I'll go to hell."?

Chapters 32-39
1. Why does Huck assume Tom Sawyer's identity?
2. What happens when Tom appears on the scene?
3. What's the difference between Tom's plan for freeing Jim and Huck's?
4. How does Huck change when Tom comes?
5. Tom's plan is actually cruel. Why?
6. What more do we learn about Tom in these chapters?

Chapters 40-43
1. How does Huck appear to be superior to Tom?
2. What happens to Jim?
3. What happens to Tom?

ANSWER KEY: STUDY GUIDE QUESTIONS - *Huckleberry Finn*

Chapters 1-3

1. Identify: Huck Finn, Tom Sawyer, Jim, Miss Watson and Widow Douglas.
    Huck Finn is the main character of the novel. Tom Sawyer is Huck's best friend and the leader of the boys' gang. Miss Watson and the Widow Douglas take care of Huck. Jim is Miss Watson's slave.

2. Why doesn't Huck get along with Miss Watson and Widow Douglas?
    Huck Finn doesn't get along with Miss Watson and Widow Douglas because they want to civilize him, and he wants to remain free.

3. What does Huck think about religion -- specifically the good place, the bad place and prayer?
    Huck doesn't believe in formal religion. If the "good place" is going to be boring, he doesn't want to go there. If his friends go to the "bad place", that is where he wants to go. Huck "don't take no stock" in prayer since it doesn't seem to do him any immediate good.

4. Give at least two examples of superstition in this section of the novel.
    Huck said that the spider's burning in the candle was bad luck. Jim talked about the witches bewitching him. Huck and the gang talk about rubbing a lamp to make a genie appear.

5. Contrast Huck and Tom. What are their main differences?
    Huck is very practical and full of common sense. Tom is a dreamer and a bookworm, full of grand ideas which are for the most part impractical.

Chapters 4-7

1. Why did Huck give his money to Judge Thatcher?
    Huck gave Judge Thatcher his money because he knew Pap Finn was coming to see him, and Pap would want all of Huck's money for buying drinks. Huck's life would be miserable and all the money would be wasted anyway.

2. Describe Pap Finn. What kind of a person is he?
    Pap was fifty years old with greasy, long, black hair. He was unshaven and had a pale white complexion. His clothes were rags. Pap was a drunk who abused Huck.

3. What is Huck's attitude towards his father?
    Huck disliked and feared Pap.

4. Why does Pap yell at Huck for becoming civilized? Is he right?
   Pap yells at Huck for becoming civilized because Huck's being civilized makes Pap feel inferior. Huck is becoming educated while Pap remains ignorant. Pap is not right to yell at Huck; he should have been proud of his son's accomplishments.

5. What was Huck's plan of escape from his father?
   Huck made it appear as if someone had broken into the cabin, murdered Huck, and dragged the body off to the river. Then Huck escaped down the river in a canoe.

6. How do you know that material things don't matter to Huck?
   Huck is always leaving material things behind. He travels light and uses whatever he can find handy to suit his needs. Also, he gave all of his money to Judge Thatcher. Material things don't mean anything to him compared to his freedom.

Chapters 8 - 11

1. What purpose(s) does Huck's death serve?
   Being "dead," Huck is truly free. He doesn't have to worry about Pap or Widow Douglas or Miss Watson coming to find him.

2. How does Huck meet Jim on Jackson's Island? Why is Jim there?
   While looking for food, Huck found a smoking campfire. Later, he set out to find who else was on the island with him. After some searching, he found Jim. Jim ran away from Miss Watson because she was going to sell him to someone from New Orleans.

3. What is in the two story house that floats by?
   A corpse was in the house. Also there were some useful items which Huck and Jim took.

4. Give three examples of Man vs. Society in this section.
   Three examples would be Huck's not liking society, Jim's not liking slavery, and Pap's attitude towards society.

5. How are the townspeople superstitious? Jim? Huck? Give examples.
   The townspeople thought that the bread would help to locate the body in the river. Jim saw the birds as a sign of rain, said counting things for dinner or shaking a tablecloth after sundown was bad luck, and said having hairy arms and breast meant you'd be rich. Huck doesn't believe that holding the snake skin would bring bad luck, but changes his mind when a snake bites Jim. (These are just some of the obvious ones.)

6. Compare/contrast Huck & Jim.
   Huck and Jim are both looking for freedom. Both have run away, and both have common sense. Both are superstitious, though Huck is a little less so than Jim. Jim is much older than Huck, almost a father-like figure, giving him advice and trying to keep him from harm.

7. Why does Huck dress as a girl to go ashore? Why does he go? What does he find out?
   Huck disguises himself as a girl to go ashore so no one would suspect his true identity. He went ashore to find out what was going on and whether the townspeople were still looking for him and Jim. He found out that people think Pap Finn or Jim may have killed Huck. There are rewards out for both Pap and Jim, and some people are going to look for Jim on Jackson's Island.

8. How do you know Huck and Jim are friends by the end of Chapter XI?
   Huck and Jim do things friends do for each other. Jim tries to protect Huck from danger and unpleasantries, and Huck tries to protect Jim from danger. They work together to help each other.

Chapters 12-14
1. Why do Huck and Jim begin their journey down the Mississippi?
   Huck and Jim begin their journey down the Mississippi when people start looking for them on Jackson's Island.

2. Why do Huck and Jim board the Walter Scott?
   Huck and Jim board the Walter Scott to investigate and to salvage goods.

3. Why does Huck want to save Jim Turner?
   Huck began to think how dreadful it was, even for murderers, to be in such a fix. He thought that one day he might be a murderer, and he wouldn't like being in that kind of a fix.

4. How does Huck send help to the Walter Scott?
   Huck went ashore and found a watchman. Huck said his family and a member of a prominent, local family were on board the wreck so the watchman would go attempt to rescue them.

5. What do we learn about Jim from his talking about "King Sollermun"?
   Through his talking about King Sollermun, Jim shows us that he thinks for himself, comes to his own conclusions, and sticks to his conclusions no matter what. We also learn that he is a very compassionate man who has a certain code of ethics.

Chapters 15-18
1. What trick does Huck play on Jim?
   Jim is asleep when Huck returns to the raft. He sits down next to Jim and pretends to be asleep. When Jim wakes up, Huck tries to make him believe that he dreamed the events of the past evening.

2. Why doesn't Huck turn in Jim?
   Huck didn't turn in Jim because they had become friends.

3. Why don't the slave hunters get Jim?
   The slave hunters don't get Jim because Huck made up a clever story about his father being ill on the raft so the hunters would not want to go near it.

4. Explain the differences between Huck and the hunters.
   The hunters were interested in collecting reward money. Huck wasn't interested in the money; he was trying to do the "right" thing. The hunters considered the runaway slaves as property; Huck considered Jim as a friend.

5. What is the bad luck in Chapter 16?
   A steamboat ran over the raft.

6. How does Huck get to the Grangerfords?
   After jumping off the raft to keep from being run over by the steamboat, Huck makes his way to the shore and comes upon the Grangerfords' house where their dogs stop him.

7. Why did Twain include this adventure with the Grangerfords?
   The Grangerfords and Shepherdsons have been feuding so long that they don't really remember why they are fighting. Twain points out how ridiculous the feud is and shows this trait of human nature as being foolish.

Chapters 19-25
1. How did Jim and Huck meet the king and duke?
   Huck went ashore to look for berries. He ran into the king and duke while they were running away from some people and dogs.

2. Does Huck believe their story?
   Huck believes the story at first, but after thinking about it, he decides that they are liars and frauds.

3. Give two examples of the "cleverness" of the king and duke.
   At the Pokeville camp meeting, the king got up and convinced the preacher to let him speak to the people. He told them that he was a pirate, now poor and reformed, who wanted to return to the Indian Ocean to reform other pirates. He asked for money for his cause, and the people gave him some.
   The duke printed up hand bills describing Jim as a runaway slave and offering a reward. He decided they would tie ropes around him to pretend they were "taking him in" so they could run the raft in the daytime.

4. Why did the people return to the show?
   People came to the show the first night to see what ladies and children were not supposed to see. After seeing the show, they didn't want to admit that they had been tricked, so they told other people in the town what a great show it was. The second show's audience

was a result of the great reviews. People came back the third night to get even with the king and duke, but the king and duke left early.

5. What's the point of the incident of the shooting of Boggs?
   The incident with Boggs points out many weaknesses in the human character. Boggs was foolish in his drunkenness to push Sherburn's patience. Sherburn was foolish to pay any attention to Boggs. The townspeople all rushed to see the murder of Boggs and almost immediately enjoyed playing the scene again. Then, the townspeople, following the lead of Buck Harkness, all decided to lynch the colonel. The colonel's speech is Twain's voice about the justice system of his time. In this section, Twain shows the worst of human nature.

6. Why do we hear about Jim's daughter "'Lizabeth"?
   Jim's story about Lizabeth shows that he is a good father and a compassionate man.

7. Where did the king and duke get their plan about being the Wilks brothers?
   The king and duke found a young man by the side of the river. He told them the story of the Wilks brothers.

Chapters 26-31

1. How do the king and duke get the money?
   The king and duke pretend to be the Wilks brothers. They take the money left to the real Wilks brothers and give it to the nieces. When the doctor calls them frauds, the nieces give the money back to the king and duke to invest for them, as a sign of their trust that they are the real Wilks brothers.

2. Why does Huck steal the money from the mattress?
   Huck stole the money back from the king and duke so that the girls would get the money which was rightfully theirs.

3. Why doesn't Huck's conscience bother him when he lies so much?
   Huck's conscience doesn't bother him when he lies because he is lying for a good cause (or for what he thinks is the right cause).

4. What things give away the king and duke?
   They don't speak very well with an English accent, their handwriting doesn't match with the real Wilks brothers' handwriting, and they don't know what was tattooed on Peter Wilks' chest.

5. Why is Huck upset when Jim is sold?
   Huck is upset when Jim is sold because Jim is his friend.

6. Why it is important that Huck says, "All right, then, I'll go to hell."?
   Huck has thought about his relationship with Jim. He has decided that Jim is his friend, and that the right thing to do is to get him out of slavery again, regardless of the consequences.

Chapters 32-39
1. Why does Huck assume Tom Sawyer's identity?
   Mrs. Phelps is expecting Tom and mistakes Huck for him, so Huck plays along.

2. What happens when Tom appears on the scene?
   When Tom comes along, Huck meets him before he reaches the house. He tells Tom what is going on. They make an arrangement about their identities, and Tom comes along to the house later, pretending to be his own brother, Sid.

3. What's the difference between Tom's plan for freeing Jim and Huck's?
   Tom's plan for freeing Jim is long and involved and like a plan from an adventure novel. Huck's plan is very practical.

4. How does Huck change when Tom comes?
   Huck lets Tom take charge since he thinks Tom knows best.

5. Tom's plan is actually cruel. Why?
   Tom's plan is cruel because Jim could be free and not worrying about his situation while he is going through the ridiculous rites Tom thinks are necessary. The rites themselves were also not very pleasant for Jim.

6. What more do we learn about Tom in these chapters?
   We learn that when Tom decides to do something, there is no changing his mind. Also he is very selfish and does not think about how his actions will affect others.

Chapters 40-43
1. How does Huck appear to be superior to Tom?
   Tom's world is a juvenile one full of pranks and dreams. Huck's world is an adult one in which he attempts to choose right from wrong and takes responsibility for his actions. Huck's common sense seems vastly superior to Tom's book learning.

2. What happens to Jim?
   Jim is set free in Miss Watson's will. Tom is ready for another adventure, but he will surely end up going home with Aunt Polly. Huck is also ready for another adventure, particularly since Aunt Sally wants to adopt and civilize him.

3. What happens to Tom?
   He goes home with Aunt Polly.

STUDY GUIDE/QUIZ QUESTIONS - *Huckleberry Finn*
Multiple Choice Format

Chapters 1-3

1. Why doesn't Huck get along with Miss Watson and Widow Douglas?
    a. Huck doesn't get along with *anyone*.
    b. They want to civilize him, and he wants to remain free.
    c. Huck's friends tell him to give the widow a hard time.
    d. Huck would rather live with Pap.

2. What does Huck think about religion -- specifically the good place, the bad place and prayer?
    a. He wants to go to the "good place" and stay away from the "bad place" but he doesn't believe in prayer.
    b. He wants to go to the "bad place" and stay away from the "good place" and he prays often.
    c. He wants to go to the "bad place" because the "good place" would be boring but he prays often.
    d. He wants to go to the "bad place" because the "good place" would be boring. He doesn't believe in prayer.

3. Which is not an example of superstition in this section of the novel.
    a. Spider burning in a candle
    b. Witches bewitched Jim.
    c. Huck walked under a ladder.
    d. Huck and the gang talk about rubbing a genie's lamp.

4. What are the main differences between Huck and Tom?
    a. Huck is practical; Tom is a dreamer.
    b. Tom is superstitious; Huck is religious.
    c. Huck is smart; Tom is not very bright.
    d. Tom is dependable; Huck is not.

Huckleberry Finn Multiple Choice Study Questions Page 2

<u>Chapters 4-7</u>

5. Why did Huck give his money to Judge Thatcher?
    a. Judge Thatcher needed a loan.
    b. Huck didn't want to have to give it to Pap, who would drink it away.
    c. Judge Thatcher was also the town's banker.
    d. He was afraid Tom would take it.

6. Describe Pap Finn. What kind of a person is he?
    a. Unshaven drunkard
    b. Pale complexion
    c. Greasy, long black hair
    d. All of the above

7. What is Huck's relationship with his father?
    a. They got along well; Pap was just too poor to keep Huck
    b. Huck loved and respected his father.
    c. Huck disliked and feared his father.
    d. Huck's father threw him out of the house because Huck was too hard to handle.

8. Why does Pap yell at Huck for becoming civilized?
    a. Pap feels inferior to his own son so he yells at him.
    b. Huck is "putting on airs" and flaunting his knowledge just to embarrass Pap.
    c. Pap doesn't really yell at Huck; it's just his way of complimenting Huck.
    d. Pap is just trying to teach Huck a valuable lesson.

9. What was Huck's plan of escape from his father?
    a. He waited for Pap to come home drunk so he could take advantage of him and escape.
    b. He waited for Pap to leave so he could cut a hole in the wall.
    c. He planned to kill Pap, but after practicing on a pig, he lost his nerve.
    d. He staged his own murder so no one would look for him.

10. How do you know that material things don't matter to Huck?
    a. He is always leaving material things behind.
    b. He travels light and uses whatever he can find to suit his needs.
    c. He gave his money to Judge Thatcher.
    d. All of the above

Huckleberry Finn Multiple Choice Study Questions Page 3

Chapters 8 -11

11. What purpose(s) does Huck's death serve?
    a. Huck "gets even" with Widow Douglas because she was so mean to him.
    b. It throws Jim and Pap together so they must depend on each other.
    c. It gives him total freedom.
    d. It shows Huck how totally dependent on civilization he has become.

12. How does Huck meet Jim on Jackson's Island?
    a. Huck saw smoke from a campfire and went to investigate.
    b. He found Jim half-drowned on the shore.
    c. Jim almost shot Huck by mistake.
    d. Huck found him in a house floating by the island.

13. What is in the two story house that floats by?
    a. A dead man
    b. Jim
    c. Tom
    d. a & c

14. Which is not an example of Man vs. Society?
    a. Pap's attitude towards government
    b. Jim's not liking slavery
    c. Huck's not liking civilization
    d. Widow Douglas's attitude towards Huck

15. What bad luck did the snakeskin bring?
    a. The bread found Huck.
    b. A snake bit Jim.
    c. All the firewood got wet.
    d. All of the above

16. How are Huck and Jim alike?
    a. Both are looking for freedom.
    b. Both are black.
    c. Neither has any relations.
    d. a & c

Huckleberry Finn Multiple Choice Study Questions Page 4

17. What is Huck's disguise to go ashore?
    a. Huck looked like a bush.
    b. Huck dressed like a slave.
    c. Huck dressed up as a girl.
    d. Huck dressed all in black so he wouldn't be seen.

18. How do you know Huck and Jim are friends by the end of Chapter XI?
    a. They try to protect each other from danger.
    b. They work together to help each other.
    c. They agree that the best thing to do would be to turn themselves in to the authorities.
    d. a & b

Huckleberry Finn Multiple Choice Study Questions Page 5

Chapters 12-14

19. Why do Huck and Jim begin their journey down the Mississippi?
    a. They've both always wanted to travel on the Mississippi.
    b. People began looking for them on Jackson's Island.
    c. A storm forces them off of the island.
    d. They just get tired of living on the island and decide to move on.

20. Why do Huck and Jim board the Walter Scott?
    a. To hide from the people who are looking for them
    b. To get in out of the rain
    c. To investigate it and salvage goods
    d. b & c

21. Why does Huck want to save Jim Turner?
    a. Huck began to think how dreadful it was, even for murderers to be in such a fix.
    b. Jim is his friend.
    c. Jim has information Huck needs.
    d. b & c

22. How does Huck send help to the Walter Scott?
    a. Huck ties an anonymous message to a brick and throws it in the window by the watchman.
    b. Huck dresses up as a girl and told Mr. Loftus to send help to the wreck.
    c. Huck sends word to Widow Douglas via Jim Turner.
    d. Huck goes ashore and tells a watchman that his family and a member of a prominent, local family are on board the wreck.

23. What do we learn about Jim from his talking about "King Sollermun"?
    a. Jim thinks for himself.
    b. Jim is compassionate.
    c. Jim is ethical.
    d. All of the above

Huckleberry Finn Multiple Choice Study Questions Page 6

Chapters 15-18

24. What trick does Huck play on Jim?
    a. He takes Jim's sleeping bag and tries to make Jim believe that witches confiscated it.
    b. He tries to make Jim believe the events of the past evening were a dream.
    c. He pretends he's going to turn Jim in to the slave hunters and even goes as far as to invite them to dinner.
    d. Huck tells Jim that the slave hunters have stopped looking for him.

25. Why doesn't Huck turn in Jim?
    a. The slave hunters leave too quickly.
    b. He figures he won't get enough of the reward money.
    c. He and Jim have become friends; he couldn't "turn in" his friend.
    d. It was too much trouble.

26. Why don't the slave hunters get Jim?
    a. Huck and Jim out-ran them.
    b. Jim was too ill to go with them.
    c. The hunters get tired of waiting and left.
    d. The hunters were afraid they would catch the disease Huck's father had.

27. Explain the differences between Huck and the hunters.
    a. The hunters wanted money; Huck wanted to do the right thing.
    b. The hunters considered Jim as property; Huck considered Jim a friend.
    c. The hunters had Jim's best interest in mind; Huck didn't want to lose his traveling companion.
    d. a & b

28. What is the bad luck in Chapter 16?
    a. Jim got sick.
    b. A steamboat ran over the raft.
    c. The hunters get Jim.
    d. Jim and Huck have an argument and split up.

29. How does Huck get to the Grangerford's?
    a. He just ended up there after jumping off the raft.
    b. Jim had told him to look for the Grangerford's place.
    c. He heard some people talking about their place along the road and decided to look for it.
    d. All of the above

Huckleberry Finn Multiple Choice Study Questions Page 7

30. Why did Twain include this adventure with the Grangerfords?
    a. Twain shows the foolish side of human nature.
    b. Twain shows Huck's determination to set Jim free.
    c. Twain shows the Grangerfords as a model family.
    d. Twain shows the Shepherdsons as a model family.

Huckleberry Finn Multiple Choice Study Questions Page 8

<u>Chapters 19-25</u>

31. How did Jim and Huck meet the king and duke?
    a. They were cousins of the Grangerfords.
    b. He bumped into them while picking berries.
    c. They came ashore in the same place he did.
    d. a & b

32. Does Huck believe their story?
    a. Not at first, but he changes his mind and does believe them..
    b. Yes, at first, but he changes his mind and thinks they're frauds.
    c. No, he never believed them.
    d. Because he was naive, he believed them right from the start and never changed his mind.

33. What shows the "cleverness" of the king and duke.
    a. They got money to reform other pirates.
    b. They tied ropes around Jim to pretend they were "taking him in."
    c. They sold twice as many tickets to their show as they had seats for and skipped town without a performance.
    d. a & b

34. Why did the people return to the show?
    a. They liked it.
    b. They didn't want to admit they'd been tricked.
    c. They came for a refund.
    d. They thought they could steal Jim and get the reward for themselves.

35. What's the point of the incident of the shooting of Boggs?
    a. It shows that there are heroes in everyday life
    b. It shows the best of human nature
    c. It points out many weaknesses in human character
    d. It furthers the subplot of Jim's quest for freedom

36. Why do we hear about Jim's daughter "'Lizabeth"?
    a. It shows Jim is a good father and compassionate man
    b. It shows Jim has no respect for family
    c. It shows that people always get what they deserve
    d. It sets up a comparison between Lizabeth and Twain's own childhood

Huckleberry Finn Multiple Choice Study Questions Page 9

37. Where did the king and duke get their plan about being the Wilks brothers?
    a. They based it on a book they read
    b. A young man by the side of the river sparked the idea
    c. Huck remembered a story Tom had told. When he told it to the king and duke, they applied it to their current situation
    d. They heard about the facts of the case in the last village they worked.

Huckleberry Finn Multiple Choice Study Questions Page 10

Chapters 26-31

38. How do the king and duke get the money?
    a. The king and duke pretend to be the Wilks brothers
    b. The king and duke sneak in and take it from the nieces.
    c. The king and duke win it from the nieces on a bet
    d. The king and duke, pretending to be the Wilks brothers, steal it from the nieces when the nieces aren't looking

39. Why does Huck steal the money from the mattress?
    a. They king and duke made him do it
    b. The real Wilks brothers made him do it
    c. He wanted to return the money to the nieces
    d. He wanted the money for himself

40. Why doesn't Huck's conscience bother him when he lies so much?
    a. His conscience never bothers him
    b. He is lying for a good cause
    c. He just doesn't think about it
    d. a & c

41. What things give away the king and duke?
    a. They don't speak well with an English accent
    b. Their handwriting doesn't match with the real Wilks brothers'
    c. They don't know what was tattooed on Peter Wilks's chest
    d. All of the above

42. Why is Huck upset when Jim is sold?
    a. Huck won't get the reward money now
    b. Jim will probably tell that he, Huck, is really alive
    c. He doesn't like the man to whom Jim is sold
    d. He will miss his friend

43. Why it is important that Huck says, "All right, then, I'll go to hell."?
    a. He has turned his back on the religion which has so often helped him
    b. He has chosen what is right according to his conscience rather than according to social or religious rules
    c. He has become such good friends with Jim that he would risk the eternal happiness of his soul to do what he thinks is right for his friend.
    d. b & c

Huckleberry Finn Multiple Choice Study Questions Page 11

Chapters 32-39

44. Why does Huck assume Tom Sawyer's identity?
    a. He admires Tom and since he can't be himself, he chooses to be Tom
    b. Mrs. Phelps mistakes him for Tom, so he plays along
    c. He wants to be able to "think like Tom" so he will know what to do in every situation
    d. He just decides to do it as he is walking down the road. He'd been thinking about Tom and it seemed like a good idea

45. What happens when Tom appears on the scene?
    a. Tom pretends to be Sid
    b. Tom pretends to be Huck
    c. Huck tells the truth and resumes his true identity
    d. None of the above

46. What's the difference between Tom's plan for freeing Jim and Huck's?
    a. Tom's is practical; Huck's is unrealistic
    b. Tom's takes less time
    c. Huck's is practical; Tom's is unrealistic
    d. Huck's is harder on Jim

47. How does Huck change when Tom comes?
    a. He becomes more bossy
    b. He lets Tom take charge
    c. He becomes moody
    d. a & c

48. Tom's plan is actually cruel. Why?
    a. Jim could be free and not worrying about his situation while he is going through the ridiculous rites Tom thinks are necessary.
    b. The rites Tom thinks up are not very pleasant for Jim
    c. a & b
    d. None of the above

49. What more do we learn about Tom in these chapters?
    a. He is selfish
    b. He is considerate
    c. He is practical when he should be
    d. He is generous

Huckleberry Finn Multiple Choice Study Questions Page 12

<u>Chapters 40-43</u>

50. How does Huck appear to be superior to Tom?
    a. Tom's world is a juvenile one full of pranks and dreams. Huck's world is an adult one in which he attempts to choose right from wrong and takes responsibility for his actions.
    b. Huck has a more aristocratic attitude.
    c. Huck's common sense seems vastly superior to Tom's book learning
    d. a & c

51. What happens to Jim?
    a. He returns as a slave to Miss Watson
    b. He is set free in Miss Watson's will
    c. He returns as a slave to Widow Douglas
    d. He volunteers to be Huck's slave because Huck as been so good to him

52. What happens to Tom?
    a. He'll probably go home with Aunt Polly
    b. He'll travel with Huck
    c. He'll probably stay with Aunt Sally
    d. He'll probably go out on his own

ANSWER KEY - MULTIPLE CHOICE STUDY/QUIZ QUESTIONS
Huckleberry Finn

<u>1 - 3</u>	<u>4 - 7</u>	<u>8 - 11</u>	<u>12 - 14</u>
1. B	5. B	11. C	19. B
2. D	6. D	12. A	20. C
3. C	7. C	13. A	21. A
4. A	8. A	14. D	22. D
	9. D	15. B	23. D
	10. D	16. A	
		17. C	
		18. D	

<u>15 - 18</u>	<u>19 - 25</u>	<u>26 - 31</u>	<u>32 - 39</u>
24. B	31. B	38. A	44. B
25. C	32. B	39. C	45. A
26. D	33. D	40. B	46. C
27. D	34. B	41. D	47. B
28. B	35. C	42. D	48. C
29. A	36. A	43. D	49. A
30. A	37. B		

<u>40 - 43</u>
50. D
51. B
52. A

PREREADING VOCABULARY WORKSHEETS

VOCABULARY - *Huckleberry Finn*

Chapter 1-3 Part I: Using Prior Knowledge and Contextual Clues

Below are the sentences in which the vocabulary words appear in the text. Read the sentence. Use any clues you can find in the sentence combined with your prior knowledge, and write what you think the underlined words mean on the lines provided.

1. ...considering how <u>dismal</u> regular and decent the widow was in all her ways, and so when I couldn't stand it no longer I lit out.

   _____

2. Well, then, the old thing <u>commenced</u> again.

   _____

3. ...you couldn't go right to eating but you had to wait for the widow to tuck down her head and grumble a little over the <u>victuals</u>...

   _____

4. "Some authorities think different but mostly it's considered best to kill them-except some that you bring to the cave here, and keep them till they're <u>ransomed</u>."

   _____

5. ...though they was only <u>lath</u> and broomsticks and you might scour at them till you rotted...

   _____

6. He said it was all done by <u>enchantment</u>.

   _____

Vocabulary - *Huckleberry Finn* Chapters 1-3 Continued

Part II: Determining the Meaning

You have tried to figure out the meanings of the vocabulary words for Chapters 1-3. Now match the vocabulary words to their dictionary definitions. If there are words for which you cannot figure out the definition by contextual clues and by process of elimination, look them up in a dictionary.

___ 1. victuals   A. free from captivity for a price
___ 2. commenced   B. food
___ 3. dismal   C. magic; sorcery
___ 4. ransomed   D. gloom or depression
___ 5. lath   E. began
___ 6. enchantment F. building material

Vocabulary - *Huckleberry Finn* Chapters 4-7

Part I: Using Prior Knowledge and Contextual Clues
    Below are the sentences in which the vocabulary words appear in the text. Read the sentence. Use any clues you can find in the sentence combined with your prior knowledge, and write what you think the underlined words mean on the lines provided.

1. I was getting sort of used to the widow's way, too, and they warn't so <u>raspy</u> on me.

_____

2. I told him I had an old slick <u>counterfeit</u> quarter that warn't no good because the brass showed through the silver a little...

_____

3. And after supper he talked to him about <u>temperance</u> and such things till the old man cried...

_____

4. ...and in the night some time he got powerful thirsty and clumb out on to the porchroof and slid down a <u>stanchion</u>...

_____

5. I took all the coffee and sugar there was all and all the ammunition; I took the <u>wadding</u>;...

_____

6. ...and people might see me and <u>hail</u> me.

_____

Part II: Determining the Meaning
    You have tried to figure out the meanings of the vocabulary words for Chapters 4-7. Now match the vocabulary words to their dictionary definitions. If there are words for which you cannot figure out the definition by contextual clues and by process of elimination, look them up in a dictionary.

  ___ 1. raspy   A. fake; not real
  ___ 2. counterfeit   B. grating; harsh
  ___ 3. temperance   C. to call to
  ___ 4. stanchion   D. post of timber or iron for support
  ___ 5. wadding   E. moderation; sobriety
  ___ 6. hail   F. material for stopping charge in a gun

Vocabulary - *Huckleberry Finn* Chapters 8-11

Part I: Using Prior Knowledge and Contextual Clues

Below are the sentences in which the vocabulary words appear in the text. Read the sentence. Use any clues you can find in the sentence combined with your prior knowledge, and write what you think the underlined words mean on the lines provided.

1. Well, then I happened to think how they always put <u>quicksilver</u> in loaves of bread and float them off...

_____

2. When they got <u>abreast</u> the head of the island they quit shooting...

_____

3. When I got to camp I warn't feeling very <u>brash</u>...

_____

4. When breakfast was ready we <u>lolled</u> on the grass...

_____

5. People will call me a low-down <u>abolitionist</u> and despise me for keeping mum...

_____

6. "What did you <u>speculate</u> in, Jim?"

_____

Part II: Determining the Meaning

You have tried to figure out the meanings of the vocabulary words for Chapters 8-11. Now match the vocabulary words to their dictionary definitions. If there are words for which you cannot figure out the definition by contextual clues and by process of elimination, look them up in a dictionary.

   ___ 1. brash   A. mercury
   ___ 2. lolled   B. person against slavery
   ___ 3. abolitionist   C. uninhibited, tactless, impudent
   ___ 4. quicksilver   D. make a risky financial transaction
   ___ 5. speculate   E. relaxed
   ___ 6. abreast   F. side by side

Vocabulary - *Huckleberry Finn* Chapters 12-14

Part I: Using Prior Knowledge and Contextual Clues

Below are the sentences in which the vocabulary words appear in the text. Read the sentence. Use any clues you can find in the sentence combined with your prior knowledge, and write what you think the underlined words mean on the lines provided.

1. It was kind of solemn, drifting down the big, still river...

_____

2. ...I seen that wreck laying there so mournful and lonesome in the middle of the river.

_____

3. ..."I can't rest, Jim, till we give her a rummaging.

_____

4. The lightning showed us the wreck again just in time, and we fetched the stabboard derrick and made it fast in time.

_____

5. But before they got in I was up in the upper berth cornered and sorry I come.

_____

Part II: Determining the Meaning

You have tried to figure out the meanings of the vocabulary words for Chapters 12-14. Now match the vocabulary words to their dictionary definitions. If there are words for which you cannot figure out the definition by contextual clues and by process of elimination, look them up in a dictionary.

___ 1. solemn   A. a crane
___ 2. mournal   B. having a respectful calm
___ 3. rummaging   C. a place to sleep
___ 4. derrick   D. sad
___ 5. berth   E. searching

Vocabulary - *Huckleberry Finn* Chapters 15-17

Part I: Using Prior Knowledge and Contextual Clues

Below are the sentences in which the vocabulary words appear in the text. Read the sentence. Use any clues you can find in the sentence combined with your prior knowledge, and write what you think the underlined words mean on the lines provided.

1. But this one was a <u>staving</u> dream.

_____

2. I'm the man with a <u>petrified</u> heart and biler-iron bowels.

_____

3. ...willing to let <u>bygones</u> be bygones.

_____

4. "'Yes,' he says, a-leaning over it, 'yes, it is my own <u>lamented</u> darling, my poor lost Charles William Allbright deceased,'...

_____

5. ...and she was leaning <u>pensive</u> on a tombstone on her right elbow under a weeping willow...

_____

6. But I reckoned that with her <u>disposition</u> she was having a better time in the graveyard.

_____

Part II: Determining the Meaning

Match the vocabulary words to their dictionary definitions. If there are words for which you cannot figure out the definition by contextual clues and by process of elimination, look them up in a dictionary.

___ 1. staving   A. grieving
___ 2. petrified   B. thoughtful
___ 3. bygones   C. past happenings
___ 4. lamented   D. inclination
___ 5. pensive   E. turned to stone
___ 6. disposition   F. put-off; delaying

Vocabulary - *Huckleberry Finn* Chapters 18-21

Part I: Using Prior Knowledge and Contextual Clues
    Below are the sentences in which the vocabulary words appear in the text. Read the sentence. Use any clues you can find in the sentence combined with your prior knowledge, and write what you think the underlined words mean.

1 "Why, nothing-only it's on account of the feud."

_____

2. I ransacked it, but couldn't find anything else.

_____

3. There was four or five men cavorting around on their horses in the open place...

_____

4., 5. ...take a turn at mesmerism and phrenology, when there's a chance...

_____

6. We want a little something to answer encores with, anyway.

_____

7. ...you can do Hamlet's soliloquy.

_____

8. Ah, it's sublime, sublime.

_____

Vocabulary - *Huckleberry Finn* Chapters 18-21 Continued

Part II: Determining the Meaning

You have tried to figure out the meanings of the vocabulary words for Chapters 18-21. Now match the vocabulary words to their dictionary definitions. If there are words for which you cannot figure out the definition by contextual clues and by process of elimination, look them up in a dictionary.

___ 1. feud   A. extravagant behavior
___ 2. ransacked   B. calls for repeat performances
___ 3. cavorting   C. reading a person's future by examining their skull
___ 4. mesmerism   D. dramatic monologue
___ 5. phrenology   E. a hereditary quarrel
___ 6. encores   F. hypnotism
___ 7. soliloquy   G. searched thoroughly but hurriedly
___ 8. sublime   H. excellent, having a sense of grandeur

Vocabulary - *Huckleberry Finn* Chapters 22-25

Part I: Using Prior Knowledge and Contextual Clues

Below are the sentences in which the vocabulary words appear in the text. Read the sentence. Use any clues you can find in the sentence combined with your prior knowledge, and write what you think the underlined words mean on the lines provided.

1. She sent out her yawl and we went aboard...

_____

2. ...but it's a trial that's sweetened and sanctified to us by this dear sympathy and these holy tears..

_____

3. ...then he blubbers out a pious goody-goody Amen, and turns himself loose and goes to crying fit to bust.

_____

4. "Poor William, afflicted as he is, his heart's aluz right."

_____

5. "I say orgies, not because it's the common term, because it ain't-obsequies being the common term-but because orgies is the right term."

_____

Part II: Determining the Meaning

You have tried to figure out the meanings of the vocabulary words for Chapters 22-25. Now match the vocabulary words to their dictionary definitions. If there are words for which you cannot figure out the definition by contextual clues and by process of elimination, look them up in a dictionary.

___ 1. yawl   A. holy
___ 2. sanctified   B. infirmed; handicapped
___ 3. pious   C. small boat
___ 4. afflicted   D. funeral rites; solemnities
___ 5. obsequies   E. religious; reverent

Vocabulary - *Huckleberry Finn* Chapters 26-28

Part I: Using Prior Knowledge and Contextual Clues

Below are the sentences in which the vocabulary words appear in the text. Read the sentence. Use any clues you can find in the sentence combined with your prior knowledge, and write what you think the underlined words mean on the lines provided.

1. . . . but I touched the curtain that hid Mary Jane's <u>frocks</u>, so I jumped in behind that and snuggled in amongst the gowns and stood there perfectly still.

_____

3. . . . so I rolled off my <u>pallet</u> and laid with my chin at the top of my ladder, and waited to see if anything was going to happen.

_____

4. The lid was shoved along about a foot, showing the dead man's face down in there, with a wet cloth over it, and his <u>shroud</u> on.

_____

5. He was the softest, glidingest, <u>stealthiest</u> man I ever see;

_____

Part II: Determining the Meaning

You have tried to figure out the meanings of the vocabulary words for Chapters 26-28. Now match the vocabulary words to their dictionary definitions. If there are words for which you cannot figure out the definition by contextual clues and by process of elimination, look them up in a dictionary.

___ 1. frock   A. a temporary bed
___ 2. pallet   B. a cloth used to wrap a body for burial
___ 3. shroud   C. having the ability to move in secret
___ 4. stealthy   D. a woman's dress

Vocabulary - *Huckleberry Finn* Chapters 29-31

Part I: Using Prior Knowledge and Contextual Clues
　　Below are the sentences in which the vocabulary words appear in the text. Read the sentence. Use any clues you can find in the sentence combined with your prior knowledge, and write what you think the underlined words mean on the lines provided.

1. Oh, he done it <u>admirable</u>.

___

2. "This is a surprise to me which I wasn't looking for; and I'll acknowledge <u>candid</u> and frank, I ain't very well fixed to meet it and answer it...

___

3. They made the king tell his yarn and they made the old gentlemen tell his'n, and anybody but a lot of <u>prejudiced</u> chuckle-heads would a'seen that the old gentleman was spinning truth and t'other one lies.

___

4. And so he warmed up and went <u>warbling</u> right along till he was actuly beginning to believe what he was saying himself, but pretty soon the new old gentleman broke in and says:

___

5. "Hold on, hold on! <u>Collar</u> all these four men and the boy, and fetch them along, too!"

___

6. ...but I didn't lose no time; and when I struck the raft at last I was so <u>fagged</u> I would 'a' just laid down to blow and gasp if I could afforded it.

___

Vocabulary - *Huckleberry Finn* Chapters 29-31 Continued

Part II: Determining the Meaning
    You have tried to figure out the meanings of the vocabulary words for Chapters 29-31. Now match the vocabulary words to their dictionary definitions. If there are words for which you cannot figure out the definition by contextual clues and by process of elimination, look them up in a dictionary.

  ___ 1. fagged   A. having a preconceived preference or idea
  ___ 2. collar   B. deserving admiration
  ___ 3. warbling   C. characterized by openness and sincerity of expression
  ___ 4. prejudiced   D. exhausted
  ___ 5. candid   E. singing
  ___ 6. admirable   F. hold onto

Vocabulary - *Huckleberry Finn* Chapters 32-33

Part I: Using Prior Knowledge and Contextual Clues
　　Below are the sentences in which the vocabulary words above appear in the text. Read the sentence. Use any clues you can find in the sentence combined with your prior knowledge, and write what you think the underlined words mean on the lines provided.

1. Yes, I remember now, he did die. Mortification set in, and they had to amputate him.

_____

2. Yes, I remember now, he did die. Mortification set in, and they had to amputate him.

_____

3. "My land!" she says, breaking in and jumping for him, "you impudent young rascal, to fool a body so-"

_____

4. "Uneasy!" she says; "I'm ready to go distracted!

_____

5. I must go up the road and waylay him.

_____

Part II: Determining the Meaning
　　You have tried to figure out the meanings of the vocabulary words for Chapters 32-33. Now match the vocabulary words to their dictionary definitions. If there are words for which you cannot figure out the definition by contextual clues and by process of elimination, look them up in a dictionary.

___ 1. impudent　　　　A. death of part of a body while the rest is alive
___ 2. mortification　　B. impertinent, offensively forward
___ 3. amputate　　　　C. to cut off
___ 4. distracted　　　　D. pulled in conflicting emotional directions
___ 5. waylay　　　　　E. to lie in wait for and attack from ambush

Vocabulary - *Huckleberry Finn* Chapters 34-39

Part I: Using Prior Knowledge and Contextual Clues

    Below are the sentences in which the vocabulary words appear in the text. Read the sentence. Use any clues you can find in the sentence combined with your prior knowledge, and write what you think the underlined words mean on the lines provided.

1. ...I couldn't see no advantage in my representing a prisoner if I got to set down and chaw over a lot of gold-leaf <u>distinctions</u> like that every time I see a chance to hog a watermelon.

   _____

2. "Huck Finn, did you *ever* hear of a prisoner having picks and shovels and all the modern <u>conveniences</u> in his wardrobe to dig himself out with?

   _____

3. "<u>Confound</u> it, it's foolish, Tom."

   _____

4. Then he went to work on the nigger, <u>coaxing</u> him and petting him and asking him if he'd been imagining he saw something again.

   _____

5. She kept a-raging right along, running her <u>insurrection</u> all by herself, and everybody else mighty meek and quiet...

   _____

6. But she counted and counted till she got that <u>addled</u> she'd start to county in the *basket* for a spoon sometimes...

   _____

7. It was most pesky <u>tedious</u> hard work and slow

   _____

8. ...and Jim'll take Aunt Sally's gown off of me and wear it and we'll all <u>evade</u> together.

   _____

Vocabulary - *Huckleberry Finn* Chapters 34-39 Continued

Part II: Determining the Meaning
    You have tried to figure out the meanings of the vocabulary words for Chapters 34-39. Now match the vocabulary words to their dictionary definitions. If there are words for which you cannot figure out the definition by contextual clues and by process of elimination, look them up in a dictionary.

  ___ 1. distinctions   A. confused
  ___ 2. conveniences   B. to obtain by persistent persuasion
  ___ 3. confound   C. the act of open revolt
  ___ 4. coaxing   D. tiresome by reason of length, slowness or dullness
  ___ 5. insurrection   E. to avoid performing
  ___ 6. addled   F. differentiation
  ___ 7. tedious   G. things that increase comfort or save work
  ___ 8. evade   H. to cause to become confused or perplexed

Vocabulary - *Huckleberry Finn* Chapters 40-43

Part I: Using Prior Knowledge and Contextual Clues

Below are the sentences in which the vocabulary words appear in the text. Read the sentence. Use any clues you can find in the sentence combined with your prior knowledge, and write what you think the underlined words mean on the lines provided.

1. But we didn't answer; we just <u>unfurled</u> our heels and shoved.

_____

2. I was just to that pass I didn't have no reasoning <u>facilities</u> no more.

_____

3. The men was very <u>huffy</u> and some of them wanted to hang Jim for an example...

_____

4. I found a good enough place for me under the bed, for it was getting pretty <u>sultry</u> for *us*, seemed to me.

_____

Part II: Determining the Meaning

You have tried to figure out the meanings of the vocabulary words for Chapters 40-43. Now match the vocabulary words to their dictionary definitions. If there are words for which you cannot figure out the definition by contextual clues and by process of elimination, look them up in a dictionary.

___ 1. unfurled   A. a fit of anger or annoyance
___ 2. faculties   B. very humid and hot
___ 3. huffy   C. spread or opened something out
___ 4. sultry   D. any of the power or capacities possessed by the human mind

ANSWER KEY: VOCABULARY - *Huckleberry Finn*

<u>1-3</u>
1. B
2. E
3. D
4. A
5. F
6. C

<u>4-7</u>
1. B
2. A
3. E
4. D
5. F
6. C

<u>8-11</u>
1. C
2. E
3. B
4. A
5. D
6. F

<u>12-14</u>
1. B
2. D
3. E
4. A
5. C

<u>15-17</u>
1. F
2. E
3. C
4. A
5. B
6. D

<u>18-21</u>
1. E
2. G
3. A
4. F
5. C
6. B
7. D
8. H

<u>22-25</u>
1. C
2. A
3. E
4. B
5. D

<u>26-28</u>
1. D
2. A
3. B
4. C

<u>29-31</u>
1. D
2. F
3. E
4. A
5. C
6. B

<u>32-33</u>
1. B
2. A
3. C
4. D
5. 5

<u>34-39</u>
1. F
2. G
3. A
4. B
5. C
6. H
7. D
8. E

<u>40-43</u>
1. C
2. D
3. A
4. B

DAILY LESSONS

LESSON ONE

Objectives
    1. To introduce the *Huckleberry Finn* unit.
    2. To distribute books and other related materials
    3. To preview the study questions for chapters 1-3
    4. To familiarize students with the vocabulary for chapters 1-3

Activity #1
    On the chalkboard write these words," Hello! How are you? What is new?"

    Have one student read the words on the board. Explain that he/she had no difficulty reading these words because they are in formal, written English. This is a common greeting one might read in a book or see in a letter.
    Introduce the idea that there are, however, many variations on this same greeting. Different people in different parts of the country (or in other English-speaking countries) say the same thing differently. In Australia, for example, one might hear, "G'day, Mate! How's it goin'?"
    Invite students to think of as many different ways of saying this same phrase as they can. Write each on the board. Spell the dialects as they sound. After you have written all the examples on the board, ask various students to read the examples. Some students will probably have trouble reading the dialects. Point out that this problem can be overcome by thinking as you read. What does this word *sound* like? What does the speaker probably mean?
    Explain to students that there are hundreds of dialects (maybe thousands!) in the English language. Some dialects will be used in *Huckleberry Finn*, the book they are about to read.

Activity #2
    Distribute the materials students will use in this unit. Explain in detail how students are to use these materials.

    Study Guides   Students should read the study guide questions for each reading assignment prior to beginning the reading assignment to get a feeling for what events and ideas are important in the section they are about to read. After reading the section, students will (as a class or individually) answer the questions to review the important events and ideas from that section of the book. Students should keep the study guides as study materials for the unit test.

    Vocabulary   Prior to reading a reading assignment, students will do vocabulary work related to the section of the book they are about to read. Following the completion of the reading of the book, there will be a vocabulary review of all the words used in the vocabulary assignments. Students should keep their vocabulary work as study materials for the unit test.

Reading Assignment Sheet　You need to fill in the reading assignment sheet to let students know by when their reading has to be completed. You can either write the assignment sheet up on a side blackboard or bulletin board and leave it there for students to see each day, or you can "ditto" copies for each student to have. In either case, you should advise students to become very familiar with the reading assignments so they know what is expected of them.

　　　Extra Activities Center　The Unit Resource section of this unit contains suggestions for an extra library of related books and articles in your classroom as well as crossword and word search puzzles. Make an extra activities center in your room where you will keep these materials for students to use. (Bring the books and articles in from the library and keep several copies of the puzzles on hand.) Explain to students that these materials are available for students to use when they finish reading assignments or other class work early.

　　　Nonfiction Assignment Sheet　Explain to students that they each are to read at least one non-fiction piece from the in-class library at some time during the unit. Students will fill out a nonfiction assignment sheet after completing the reading to help you (the teacher evaluate their reading experiences and to help the students think about and evaluate their own reading experiences. The nonfiction reading assignment in this unit is incorporated into the Group Theme Project.

　　　Books　Each school has its own rules and regulations regarding student use of school books. Advise students of the procedures that are normal for your school.

　　　Theme Project　This unit comes with a theme project for students to complete. You will divide your class into five groups, one for each of five main themes in the book. Students will work within their own themes throughout the unit and will create class-period-long presentations relating their themes, to be presented as culminating activities near the end of the unit. Distribute the Theme Project Assignment Sheets and the related papers. Discuss this activity in detail.

Activity #3
　　　Preview the study questions and have students do the vocabulary work for Chapters 1-3 of *Huckleberry Finn*. If students do not finish this assignment during this class period, they should complete it prior to the next class meeting.

GROUP THEME PROJECT ASSIGNMENT
Huckleberry Finn

PROMPT

As you read the book *Huckleberry Finn*, you will notice that certain ideas or themes keep popping up over and over again. Five of the main themes are freedom, religion, superstition, education, and nature.

Your class has been (or will shortly be) divided up into five groups, one group for each of the above-mentioned themes. You will do a series of assignments relating to the theme you have been assigned, and the assignments will all lead towards a final class-period-long presentation your group will create and present.

Put away your ideas of a stuffy, practically dusty, old-time, boring presentation. Nope. We'll have none of that. Your presentation will be a one-of-a-kind masterpiece filled with your own interesting ideas combined with knowledge you gain from collecting information from various sources and presented with your skillful use of modern technology.

DESCRIPTION

Your project is divided into several parts. A description of each part follows:

* Part One: This first part is an important base for the rest of your work. You are to keep a journal. (Don't groan!) As you read the book *Huckleberry Finn*, keep a record of all the references to your theme that you can find. Jot down the chapter and page numbers and a brief summary of the reference. For example, "Chapter 6, pages 55-57, Huck is kept prisoner by his father" could be a sample entry for the theme of freedom. In another section of your journal, keep a little list of your own thoughts and things you have heard about that relate to your theme, either in fiction or in real life. The last pages of your journal will pull together all of your fragmented references and will incorporate many of your ideas. See Writing Assignment #1 for complete instructions.

*Part Two: There is a saying that art imitates life; in other words, what we read in books, see in movies, or hear in our music reflects the things that are (or were) going on in real life. Examining real life, then, is the point to examining books, movies, or music. We look at and listen to these things to better understand our world and ourselves. In Part One, we dealt mostly with the book. In Part Two, we will deal mostly with the real world. Your assignment in Part Two is to look at your theme in our world today. What things, what issues, what topics, what ideas in our world today relate to your theme? Your group will brainstorm a list of ways your theme relates to our world today. You will then divide up your list and go get some facts to back up and fill out your ideas. See the Making It Relevant page for complete instructions.

* Part Three: You have looked at your theme both in the text and in real life. Now you need to create a presentation to convey all the ideas you have gathered. Your presentations must include information from the text you read (*Huck Finn*) and information from your "real world" pool of ideas. See Presentation Guidelines for complete instructions.

WRITING ASSIGNMENT #1 - *Huckleberry Finn*

PROMPT

In your journal, you have kept two kinds of information: a list of references to your theme in the text and a list of ideas you have had about your theme. After you have finished reading the book and have finished making your journal entries, you are to write a composition about your theme as it relates to the book.

PREWRITING

Most of your prewriting has been done already through the work you did in your journal. Now it is time for you to analyze the data you have collected while you were reading. Go back and read through all of your journal entries.

Freedom: Do all of your entries deal with the same kinds of freedom or are there examples of many kinds of freedom/bondage? What different kinds are there? Note which of your examples in your journal support which different aspects of freedom/bondage. After you have grouped them, look at your data for each set. What does each set of examples seem to be showing?

Religion: If you look carefully at your journal entries, you will probably see that different characters in the book have different opinions about religion, and through those characters, Twain also gives his opinions. Categorize your data by characters. After you have done so, look at the examples of what each character says or does relating to the theme of religion. Jot down your notes about each character's views on the topic. What do you think Twain's view is?

Superstition: Most of the references to superstitions in the book are put forth by Huck and Jim. Group your examples accordingly. Look at your examples, then, for each character. What are Huck's attitudes towards superstitions? What are Jim's?

Education: As you look at your examples in your journal, you will probably see that there are two main ideas presented about this topic. Some characters think book learning is more important than practical knowledge from/about life experiences, and some characters think vice versa. Group your data into these two categories. Then, make notes about which characters believe schooling is more important and which characters believe practical knowledge from life experiences is more important. What do you think Twain believed?

Huck Finn Writing Assignment #1 Page 2

    Nature: There is a basic conflict between nature and civilization. Look at your data references to nature. What kinds of things happen when the characters are in nature, away from civilization? Think back to the story and jot down a few notes about what things happen when the characters are back in "civilization." Judging from this data, what do you think Twain was perhaps trying to tell us about nature, civilization, and people?

DRAFTING

    Freedom: Write an introductory paragraph explaining that there are several different kinds of freedom/bondage shown in the novel *Huckleberry Finn*. Specify what they are. In the body of your paper, write one paragraph for each of the different types you found. As a format for each paragraph, you could make a statement about the kind of freedom/bondage you will discuss in the paragraph and then use the examples you found in the book to support and explain your statement. After you have completed the paragraphs in the body of your composition, write a concluding paragraph (based on the information you have just presented) explaining what you think Twain intended to point out about the theme of freedom.

    Religion: Write an introductory paragraph in which you explain that religion is one of the major themes in the novel *Huckleberry Finn* and point out that Twain has given the characters in the book definite opinions on the subject through which Twain's own opinions can be heard. In the body of your paper, write one paragraph for each character who has opinions about religion. Write a topic sentence stating who the character is and what his/her opinion of religion seems to be. Use the specific examples you found in the text to support your statements. Then write a concluding paragraph in which you tell what you think Twain's opinion was, based on the information you have just set forth.

    Superstition: Your composition can probably most easily be written as a comparison-contrast essay comparing and contrasting the views Huck and Jim have of superstitions. Write an introductory paragraph in which you introduce the idea that superstition is one of the themes in the novel and that most of the theme is developed through Huck and Jim. State briefly the main way(s) their attitudes towards superstitions are different. In the body of your paper, take (at least) one paragraph to explore Jim's attitudes towards superstitions and (at least) one paragraph to discuss Huck's attitudes about it. Use the specific examples you have gathered to support your statements. Then write a concluding paragraph in which you tell what you think Twain was trying to point out through his use of superstition in the book.

Huck Finn Writing Assignment #1 Page 3

Education: Write an introductory paragraph in which you introduce the idea that one of the conflicts the story is book learning versus practical knowledge from life experiences and that Twain uses his characters to set forth his views on this topic. In the body of your composition, write one paragraph for each character about whom you have collected data. Write a topic sentence telling that character's views about education and then use examples from the text you have collected to support your statement. In your concluding paragraph, tell what you think Twain's point was about education, based on the information you have just compiled.

Nature: Write an introductory paragraph in which you introduce the idea that nature versus civilization is one of the main conflicts in *Huckleberry Finn*. Write one paragraph in which you detail what kinds of events take place in nature in the story and then one paragraph in which you detail what kinds of things happen in civilization. In your concluding paragraph, explain what you think Twain was trying to tell us through the actions of his characters.

<u>PROMPT</u>

When you finish the rough draft of your paper, ask a student who sits near you to read it. After reading your rough draft, he/she should tell you what he/she liked best about your work, which parts were difficult to understand, and ways in which your work could be improved. Reread your paper considering your critic's comments and make the corrections you think are necessary.

MAKING IT RELEVANT
Huck Finn Project Assignment Part II

PROMPT
You have read enough of the book *Huckleberry Finn* and have made enough journal entries to get some ideas about your theme in the book. Now take a look at that theme in real life. In this part of your project, you will be brainstorming and gathering information for the "real life" portion of your presentation.

HOW TO BEGIN
Get together with the other members of your group. Brainstorm a list of ideas of current topics that relate to your theme. If you get stuck (or perhaps in preparation for your group discussion), ask your parents, neighbors, friends, etc. what current topics might be appropriate for your theme. If you are still stuck, go to the library and look in the guide to periodicals. That should have a lot of suggestions.

WHAT TO DO NEXT
You have a list of topics. Decide which topics you think will work best for your presentation. Which topics do you think will have the most written and visual information readily available for you? Which topics most interest you? Narrow your list down to one topic for each of your group members.

GET THE FACTS
Each group member needs to gather information about his/her topic.

Go to the library and find a bunch of articles from various publications and read them. Take notes. Be sure to identify the source of your notes somewhere on your page so you know from where your information came. If your topic is broad, find information about many different aspects of it so your information is well-rounded.

Don't limit yourself to the library and periodicals. Check for videos, news clips from your local TV station, posters, or other materials available from agencies related to your topics. Interview real, live people who are knowledgeable about your topic. If you do interviews with real people, take a video camera along. That will help give you more materials for your presentation. You are an investigative reporter uncovering as much material as you can for your story. Take video pictures of things in your area that relate to your topic. Be active! You are Diane Sawyer or Barbara Walters or Sam Donaldson or Ed Bradley. Do you think they just half-heartedly browse through a few old, stuffy periodicals? No way! Get the latest scoop!

Keep in mind that you will have to make a presentation to the class. In that presentation you will have to use visual materials. Be on the lookout for things that could possibly be used.

PUT IT TOGETHER

Look at all the stuff you've found! You have notes from articles, some great pictures, some video footage or sound recordings from newscasts, and who knows what else--other goodies you were able to scoop up. What to do with it all? Weed and organize. Weed out the things that are not important and keep the things that are essential for your story. Organize the things you decide to keep so that you have a compact nucleus of material that explains the essence of your topic.

After each group member has done his research (and weeded and organized it), get back together as a group to look at the entire body of research that has been done. Evaluate your work yourselves.

PRESENTATION GUIDELINES
Huck Finn Project Assignment Part III

PROMPT

You have taken a close look at your theme in the text and in real life. Now it is time to put it all together into a presentation. You are no longer an investigative reporter; you are a director, editor and producer of a prime-time television special about your topic.

REQUIREMENTS

1. This must be a multi-media presentation. That is, you can't just stand up there in front of the class and read a boring report to the class. You must incorporate audio or visual materials -- photos, drawings, charts, maps, video tapes, and/or models, sound recordings -- you can even dress up as the characters if you want to -- anything that will give some life to your presentation.

2. Every group member must have at least one specific assignment contributing to the production and/or presentation of your project.

3. You must include information about your topic in the text, information about your topic in real life, and a closing which summarizes your main points and ties the two portions of your presentation together if possible.

4. Your presentation must last between ____ and ____ minutes.

Note: These are not the only things on which you will be graded, but they are the basic requirements for the assignment. You will also be graded on how well these requirements are fulfilled, how thoroughly you cover your topic, and how well you actually do your presentation.

HOW TO BEGIN

Get together in your group. You have two main bodies of information to work with in your presentation: your topic in the text and your topic in real life. Look at all the information you have gathered. The best way to organize your presentation is probably to present all the information about the text and then present all the information about real life (or vice-versa) and then have a short summary connecting the two if possible.

PUTTING IT TOGETHER
There's no way to do this but to roll up your sleeves and dig in.

1. Answer these questions:
    How much time do you have for your total presentation?
    How much time will you allow for the portion of the presentation about the text?
    How much time will you allow for the portion of the presentation about real life?
    How much time will you allow for the summary/closing?

2. Will you present the text portion first or the real life portion first?

3. Organize your first portion of the presentation by making an outline.
    What points do you want to make about your topic in the text?
    What materials do you have available (or can you create) to make these points?
    In what order will it be best to present these materials? (Make your outline.)
    Check to make sure you can present these materials in the time allotted.

4. Organize your second portion of the presentation by making an outline.
    What related current topics do you want to present?
    What materials do you have available (or can you create) to make these points?
    In what order will it be best to present these materials? (Make your outline.)
    Check to make sure you can present these materials in the time allotted.

5. Make a list of things that need to be done for your presentation. Assign tasks to each group member.

6. Do the tasks that are assigned.

7. Have a "dress rehearsal" of your presentation if you have time.

NONFICTION ASSIGNMENT SHEET
(To be completed after reading the required nonfiction article)

Name _____ Date _____

Title of Nonfiction Read _____

Written By _____ Publication Date _____

I. Factual Summary: Write a short summary of the piece you read.

II. Vocabulary
    1. With which vocabulary words in the piece did you encounter some degree of difficulty?

    2. How did you resolve your lack of understanding with these words?

III. Interpretation: What was the main point the author wanted you to get from reading his work?

IV. Criticism
    1. With which points of the piece did you agree or find easy to accept? Why?

    2. With which points of the piece did you disagree or find difficult to believe? Why?

V. Personal Response: What do you think about this piece? OR How does this piece influence your ideas?

LESSON TWO

Objectives
1. To read chapters 1-3
2. To give students practice reading orally
3. To evaluate students' oral reading

Activity

Have students read chapters 1-3 of *Huckleberry Finn* out loud in class. You probably know the best way to get readers with your class; pick students at random, ask for volunteers, or use whatever method works best for your group. If you have not yet completed an oral reading evaluation for your students this marking period, this would be a good opportunity to do so. A form is included with this unit for your convenience.

If your students have a hard time with the dialect, sometimes reading the first chapter or two to them helps. That way, they hear some of the most common words they will encounter in their reading before they have to face those words on their own. A tape recording of *Huckleberry Finn* is available from CAEDMON, 1995 Broadway, New York, NY 10023. Other versions are available as well.

If students do not complete reading chapters 1-3 in class, they should do so prior to your next class meeting.

ORAL READING EVALUATION - *Huckleberry Finn*

Name _____ Class____ Date _____

SKILL	EXCELLENT	GOOD	AVERAGE	FAIR	POOR
Fluency	5	4	3	2	1
Clarity	5	4	3	2	1
Audibility	5	4	3	2	1
Pronunciation	5	4	3	2	1
_____	5	4	3	2	1
_____	5	4	3	2	1

Total _____   Grade _____

Comments:

LESSON THREE

Objectives
1. To review the main events and ideas from chapters 1-3
2. To preview the study questions for chapters 4-7
3. To familiarize students with the vocabulary in chapters 4-7
4. To read chapters 4-7

Activity #1
Give students a few minutes to formulate answers for the study guide questions for chapters 1-3 and then discuss the answers to the questions in detail. Write the answers on the board or overhead transparency so students can have the correct answers for study purposes. NOTE: It is a good practice in public speaking and leadership skills for individual students to take charge of leading the discussions of the study questions. Perhaps a different student could go to the front of the class and lead the discussion each day that the study questions are discussed during this unit. Of course, the teacher should guide the discussion when appropriate and be sure to fill in any gaps the students leave.

Activity #2
Give students about fifteen minutes to preview the study questions for chapters 4-7 of *Huckleberry Finn* and to do the related vocabulary work.

Activity #3
Assign students to read chapters 4-7 of *Huckleberry Finn* prior to your next class period. If there is time remaining in this period, students may begin reading silently.

LESSON FOUR

Objectives
    1. To check to see that students read chapters 4-7 as assigned
    2. To review the main ideas and events from chapters 4-7
    3. To preview the study questions for chapters 8-11
    4. To familiarize students with the vocabulary in chapters 8-11
    5. To read chapters 8-11
    6. To evaluate students' oral reading

Activity #1
    Quiz - Distribute quizzes and give students about 10 minutes to complete them. (NOTE: The quizzes may either be the short answer study guides or the multiple choice version.) Have students exchange papers. Grade the quizzes as a class. Collect the papers for recording the grades. (If you used the multiple choice version as a quiz, take a few minutes to discuss the answers for the short answer version if your students are using the short answer version for their study guides.)

Activity #2
    Give students about 15 minutes to preview the study questions for chapters 8-11 and to do the related vocabulary work.

Activity #3
    Have students read chapters 8-11 orally for the remainder of the class period. Continue the oral reading evaluations. If students do not complete reading these chapters during this class period, they should do so prior to your next class meeting.

LESSON FIVE

Objectives
    1. To review the main ideas and events from chapters 8-11
    2. To do the prereading work for chapters 12-14
    3. To read chapters 12-14
    4. To point out several words and phrases (in chapters 1-11) that have different usages or meanings from current usages or meanings

Activity #1
    Give students a few minutes to formulate answers for the study guide questions for chapters 8-11, and then discuss the answers to the questions in detail. Write the answers on the board or overhead transparency so students can have the correct answers for study purposes.

Activity #2
    Distribute the Language Usage Worksheets. Discuss the directions in detail and give students ample time to complete the assignment. When students have finished, discuss the answers with your class.

Activity #3
    Tell students that prior to Lesson Seven (give students a day and a date) they should have completed the prereading work and the reading of chapters 12-14. If there is time left in this class period, students may begin to work on this assignment.

LESSON SIX

Objectives
    To give students time to work on their group theme projects

Activity
    Give students this class period to work on their group theme projects. Students should discuss the references they have found to their themes in the novel so far, brainstorm applications of their themes to life today, and set up specific topics to research in Lesson Ten.

LANGUAGE USAGE WORKSHEET
Huckleberry Finn

Below is a passage from *The Adventures of Huckleberry Finn*. Your assignment is to rewrite it in proper, standard English. Read through the passage at least twice, underlining or highlighting all of the mistakes you can find as you read. Then rewrite the passage, fixing the errors.

You don't know about me without you have read a book by the name of *The Adventures of Tom Sawyer*; but that ain't no matter. That book was made by Mr. Mark Twain, and he told the truth, mainly. There was things which he stretched, but mainly he told the truth. That is nothing. I never seen anybody but lied one time or another, without it was Aunt Polly, or the widow, or maybe Mary. Aunty Polly–Tom's Aunt Polly, she is–and Mary, and the Widow Douglas is all told about in that book, which is mostly a true book, with some stretchers, as I said before.

Now the way that book winds up is this: Tom and me found the money that the robbers hid in the cave, and it made us rich. We got six thousand dollars apiece–all gold. It was an awful sight of money when it was piled up. Well, Judge Thatcher he took it and put it out at interest, and it fetched us a dollar a day apiece all the year round–more than a body could tell what to do with. The Widow Douglas she took me for her son, and allowed she would sivilize me; but it was rough living in the house all the time, considering how dismal regular and decent the widow was in all her ways; and so when I couldn't stand it no longer I lit out. I got into my old rags and my sugar-hogshead again, and was free and satisfied. But Tom Sawyer he hunted me up and said he was going to start a band of robbers, and I might join if I would go back to the widow and be respectable. So I went back.

The widow she cried over me, and called me a poor lost lamb, and she called me a lot of other names, too, but she never meant no harm by it. She put me in them new clothes again, and I couldn't do nothing but sweat, and feel all cramped up. Well, then, the old thing commenced again. The widow rung a bell for supper, and you had to come to time. When you got to the table you couldn't go right to eating, but you had to wait for the widow to tuck down her head and grumble a little over the victuals, though there warn't really anything the matter with them–that is, nothing only everything was cooked by itself. In a barrel of odds and ends it is different; things get mixed up, and the juice kind of swaps around, and the things go better.

After supper she got out her book and learned me about Moses and the Bulrushers, and I was in a sweat to find out all about him; but by and by she let it out that Moses had been dead a considerable long time; so then I didn't care no more about him, because I don't take no stock in dead people.

LANGUAGE USAGE WORKSHEET ANSWER KEY
Huck Finn

There can be many different revisions of this passage depending on how much of the flavor of the passage you want to leave in or take out. One of the interesting aspects of doing this exercise is trying to decide which phrases should be used in "proper English" and which ones should not. Does "proper English" include colloquialisms? A businessman using "proper English" telling a similar story about his childhood would never use some of the phrases that Huck uses here. Does that mean that these phrases are not "proper English"? Some corrections are black and white: the subject and the verb have to agree, double negatives are unacceptable, and words must be spelled correctly. Things that break hard and fast rules of English are easy to spot. But, there are many gray areas in this passage. What is a run-on sentence? Exactly how should it be rewritten? What is a matter of style or meaning as opposed to correct usage? After students write their own revisions (individually or in small groups), discuss with them which things in the passage *must* be changed, which things probably *should* be changed, which things *could* be changed, and *why*.

You don't know about me unless you have read a book by the name of *The Adventures of Tom Sawyer*, but that doesn't matter. That book was written by Mr. Mark Twain, and he mainly told the truth. There were things which he stretched, but mainly he told the truth. I never saw anybody who didn't lie at one time or another, unless it was Aunt Polly, or the widow, or maybe Mary. Aunt Polly–who is actually Tom's Aunt Polly–and Mary, and the Widow Douglas are all told about in that book, which is mostly a true book with some stretchers, as I said before.

At the end of *The Adventures of Tom Sawyer*, Tom and I found the money that the robbers had hidden in the cave, and it made us rich. We each got six thousand dollars–all gold. It was quite a sight when it was all piled up! Well, Judge Thatcher took it and put it out at interest. Tom and I got a dollar a day each all the year around, which was more than we knew what to do with. [Note: *Technically this sentence should not end in a preposition; however, rephrasing the clause while maintaining the words and intent of the clause is very awkward, so we have chosen to leave the word "with" at the end. You might discuss this problem with your students and see what alternatives they create.*] The Widow Douglas took me for her son and said she would civilize me. But my living in the house all the time was rough, considering how regular and decent the widow was in all her ways. When I couldn't stand it any longer, I left. I changed into my old clothes again and was free and satisfied. However, Tom Sawyer found me and told me that he was going to start a band of robbers and that I could join if I would go back to the widow and be respectable. So I went back.

The widow cried over me and called me a poor lost lamb, and she called me many other names, too, but she didn't mean any harm by that. She dressed me in those new clothes again, and I couldn't do anything but sweat and feel all cramped. Well, then, the old thing commenced again. The widow rang a bell for supper, and I had to come right away. When I got to the table, I couldn't start eating right away. I had to wait for the widow to tuck down her head and grumble a little over the victuals, though there wasn't really anything the matter with them; that is, nothing except each thing was cooked by itself. In a barrel of odds and ends, things get mixed up and the juice swaps around, and the things taste better.

After supper, the Widow Douglas got out her book and taught me about Moses and the Bulrushers. I was very interested to find out all about him, but eventually the widow told me that Moses had been dead a considerably long time. Then I didn't care any more about him because I don't take any stock in dead people.

LESSON SEVEN

Objectives
>   1. To review the main events of chapters 12-14
>   2. To check to see that students did the reading assignment
>   3. To assign the pre-reading, vocabulary and reading work for chapters 15-18

Activity #1
>   Give students a quiz on chapters 12-14. Use either the short answer or multiple choice form of the study guide questions as a quiz so that in discussing the answers to the quiz you also answer the study guide questions. Collect the papers for grade recording.

Activity #2
>   Tell students that prior to their next class period, they must have completed the pre-reading, vocabulary and reading work for chapters 15-18. Students may have the remainder of this period to work on this assignment.

LESSON EIGHT

Objectives
>   1. To review the main ideas and events of chapters 15-18
>   2. To preview the study questions for chapters 19-25
>   3. To do the vocabulary work for chapters 19-25
>   4. To read chapters 19-25

Activity #1
>   Discuss the answers to the study guide questions for chapters 15-18. Write the answers on the board for students to copy down for study use later.

Activity #2
>   Tell students that prior to your next class period, they should have completed the prereading and reading work for chapters 19-25. If time remains in this class period, they may begin working on this assignment.

LESSON NINE

Objectives
>   1. To review the main ideas and events from chapters 19-25
>   2. To preview the study questions and vocabulary for chapters 26-31
>   3. To read chapters 26-31

Activity
>   Discuss the answers to the study guide questions for chapters 19-25. Write the answers on the board for students to copy for study use later. Tell students that prior to your next class period, they should have completed the prereading and reading work for chapters 26-31. Students may use the remainder of this class period to begin working on this assignment.

LESSON TEN

Objectives
> 1. To review the main ideas and events from chapters 26-31
> 2. To give students time to work on their group theme projects

Activity #1
> Discuss the answers to the study guide questions for chapters 26-31. Write the answers on the board for students to copy for study use later.

Activity #2
> Take students to the library and give them the remainder of this class period to work on their group theme projects. In this class period they should be doing the research to find articles, news clips, videos, etc. about topics relating their theme to our world today.

LESSON ELEVEN

Objectives
> 1. To preview the study questions and vocabulary for chapters 32-39
> 2. To read chapters 32-39

Activity #1
> Give students about fifteen minutes to do the prereading work for chapters 32-39.

Activity #2
> Tell students that prior to your next class period they should have read chapters 32-39. Students may use the remainder of this class period to work on this assignment.

LESSON TWELVE

Objectives
> 1. To review the main ideas and events from chapters 32-39
> 2. To preview the study questions and vocabulary for chapters 40-43
> 3. To read chapters 40-43

Activity #1
> Discuss the answers to the study guide questions for chapters 32-39. Write the answers on the board for students to copy for study use later.

Activity #2
> Give students about fifteen minutes to do the prereading work for chapters 40-43.
> Tell students that prior to your next class period they should have read chapters 40-43. Students may use the remainder of this class period to work on this assignment.

LESSON THIRTEEN

Objectives
    1. To review the main ideas and events from chapters 40-43
    2. To give students time to work on their group theme projects

Activity #1
    Discuss the answers to the study guide questions for chapters 40-43. Write the answers on the board for students to copy for study use later.

Activity #2
    Give students the remainder of this class period to work on their group theme projects. During this class, they should be reviewing and compiling their research from Lesson Ten and brainstorming plans for making their presentations.

LESSON FOURTEEN

Objectives
    1. To give students the opportunity to practice writing to express their personal opinions
    2. To give the teacher the opportunity to evaluate students' writing skills
    3. To give students the opportunity to think about themselves, their own personalities
    4. To analyze and review the characters in the novel

Activity
    Distribute Writing Assignment #2. Discuss the directions in detail and give students the remainder of the class period to do the assignment. Collect the papers at the end of your class period.

WRITING ASSIGNMENT #2 - *Huckleberry Finn*

PROMPT

We have been working with the themes in the novel *Huckleberry Finn*; now let's look at the characters. There are many different characters in this book. Your assignment is to choose one character you think you are most like and explain why you think you are most like that character.

PREWRITING

Make a list of all the characters in the book. Next to each one, write down two or three of their most characteristic personality traits. Make a list of several of your own personality traits. Then decide which of the characters has personality traits closest to your own. Are you sneaky like the King and the Duke, or are you a daydreaming, romantic reader like Tom? Maybe you feel more like Pap Finn: you think education is a waste of time and prefer to stay drunk all your life! These are just a few of the many examples you will have to choose from after your list is complete.

DRAFTING

Write an introductory paragraph in which you introduce the idea that you and your character from *Huckleberry Finn* have certain traits in common.

In the body of your paper, devote one paragraph to each of the traits you have chosen. Write a topic sentence in which you make clear what trait the paragraph will be about. Follow that with examples of how the character shows this trait and ways in which you show the trait as well.

Write a concluding paragraph in which you determine just how much you and your character are alike.

PROMPT

When you finish the rough draft of your paper, ask a student who sits near you to read it. After reading your rough draft, he/she should tell you what he/she liked best about your work, which parts were difficult to understand, and ways in which your work could be improved. Reread your paper considering your critic's comments and make the corrections you think are necessary.

PROOFREADING

Do a final proofreading of your paper double-checking your grammar, spelling, organization, and the clarity of your ideas.

LESSON FIFTEEN

Objective
    To review all of the vocabulary work done in this unit

Activity
    Choose one (or more) of the vocabulary review activities listed below and spend your class period as directed in the activity. Some of the materials for these review activities are located in the Extra Activities section in this unit.

VOCABULARY REVIEW ACTIVITIES

1. Divide your class into two teams and have an old-fashioned spelling or definition bee.

2. Give each of your students (or students in groups of two, three or four) a *Huckleberry Finn* Vocabulary Word Search Puzzle. The person (group) to find all of the vocabulary words in the puzzle first wins.

3. Give students a *Huckleberry Finn* Vocabulary Word Search Puzzle without the word list. The person or group to find the most vocabulary words in the puzzle wins.

4. Use a *Huckleberry Finn* Vocabulary Crossword Puzzle. Put the puzzle onto a transparency on the overhead projector (so everyone can see it), and do the puzzle together as a class.

5. Give students a *Huckleberry Finn* Vocabulary Matching Worksheet to do.

6. Divide your class into two teams. Use the *Huckleberry Finn* vocabulary words with their letters jumbled as a word list. Student 1 from Team A faces off against Student 1 from Team B. You write the first jumbled word on the board. The first student (1A or 1B) to unscramble the word wins the chance for his/her team to score points. If 1A wins the jumble, go to student 2A and give him/her a definition. He/she must give you the correct spelling of the vocabulary word which fits that definition. If he/she does, Team A scores a point, and you give student 3A a definition for which you expect a correctly spelled matching vocabulary word. Continue giving Team A definitions until some team member makes an incorrect response. An incorrect response sends the game back to the jumbled-word face off, this time with students 2A and 2B. Instead of repeating giving definitions to the first few students of each team, continue with the student after the one who gave the last incorrect response on the team. For example, if Team B wins the jumbled-word face-off, and student 5B gave the last incorrect answer for Team B, you would start this round of definition questions with student 6B, and so on. The team with the most points wins!

7. Have students write a story in which they correctly use as many vocabulary words as possible. Have students read their compositions orally! Post the most original compositions on your bulletin board.

LESSON SIXTEEN

Objectives
    To discuss *Huckleberry Finn* on interpretive and critical levels

Activity #1
    Choose the questions from the Extra Discussion Questions/Writing Assignments which seem most appropriate for your students. A class discussion of these questions is most effective if students have been given the opportunity to formulate answers to the questions prior to the discussion. To this end, you may either have all the students formulate answers to all the questions, divide your class into groups and assign one or more questions to each group, or you could assign one question to each student in your class. The option you choose will make a difference in the amount of class time needed for this activity.

Activity #2
    After students have had ample time to formulate answers to the questions, begin your class discussion of the questions and the ideas presented by the questions. Be sure students take notes during the discussion so they have information to study for the unit test.

LESSON SEVENTEEN

Objectives
    1. To give students time to make final preparations for their group presentations
    2. To give students feedback about their writing skills

Activity #1
    Give students this class period to work on their group theme projects. During this class period, students should be making their final preparations for their presentations. They should have their materials gathered, their presentations planned, and should just be putting the finishing touches on their projects and doing a "dress rehearsal."

Activity #2
    While students are working in their groups, call students to your desk or some other private area for a writing evaluation conference. Discuss students' strengths and weaknesses in their writing based on Writing Assignment #1 and Writing Assignment #2. An evaluation form is included with this unit for your convenience.

EXTRA WRITING ASSIGNMENTS/DISCUSSION QUESTIONS - *Huckleberry Finn*

Interpretation

1. Explain why Mark Twain used Huck as the narrator.

2. If you were to rewrite *Huckleberry Finn* as a play, where would you start and end each act? Explain why.

3. What are the main conflicts in the story? Are all the conflicts resolved? Explain how those that are resolved are resolved, and explain why those that are not resolved are not.

4. Explain the importance and influence of the setting(s) in the novel.

5. Which characters are "good guys" and which characters are "bad guys"? Explain your choices.

Critical

6. Compare and contrast Huck's relationship with Pap with his relationship with Widow Douglas.

7. Are Huck's actions believably motivated? Explain why or why not.

8. Does Huck develop or change as a result of his adventures? Explain how he does if he does, or why he does not if he does not.

9. How does Mark Twain's humor contribute to the value of the novel? Give specific examples.

10. Compare and contrast Tom and Huck.

11. Describe Huck's relationship with Jim

12. The King and Duke figure prominently in a whole section of the book. Why did Twain include them?

13. What is *satire*? Give several examples of Twain's use of satire in *Huckleberry Finn*.

14. Explain Tom's role in the novel. Why was he included?

15. The only information we receive about the characters in the novel, we receive from Huck. Yet we seem to know more about them than Huck does. Choose two characters and explain how Twain achieves this effect.

Huckleberry Finn Extra Discussion Questions page 2

16. Are the characters in *Huckleberry Finn* stereotypes? If so, explain why Mark Twain used stereotypes. If not, explain how the characters merit individuality.

17. Discuss the importance and the role of these characters in *Huckleberry Finn*: the Grangerfords, Jim Turner, Col. Sherburn, Aunt Sally, and Pap.

Critical/Personal Response

18. Is the story of *Huckleberry Finn* believable? Explain why or why not.

19. Why did Twain write about a boy and the Mississippi River?

20. How would the story and its effect have changed if Pap had lived? If Jim had not been set free?

21. Do you think the relationship between Huck and Jim is realistic? Explain why or why not.

22. Are there people like the King and Duke in our world today? If so, what are some examples of their types?

Personal Response

23. Did you enjoy reading *Huckleberry Finn*? Why or why not?

24. If Huck had written a poem while floating down the Mississippi, what do you think it would have been? Write the poem as you think Huck would have written it.

27. Are there people in your neighborhood who are like any of the character types in the novel? Change the real person's name so his/her identity remains anonymous and describe how he or she is like a particular character.

28. If Huck were living today, where would he live and what would he be doing?

29. What does it mean to be "educated"? Which, if either, do you think is more important: book learning or practical life experiences?

30. What is freedom? Is anyone really, truly free?

31. Do you believe in superstitions? If so, what kinds? If not, why not?

WRITING EVALUATION FORM - *Huck Finn*

Name _____ Date _____

Grade _____

Circle One For Each Item:

Grammar: corrections noted on paper

Spelling: corrections noted on paper

Punctuation: corrections noted on paper

Legibility: excellent   good   fair   poor

_____   excellent   good   fair   poor

_____   excellent   good   fair   poor

Strengths:

Weaknesses:

Comments/Suggestions:

LESSONS EIGHTEEN TO TWENTY-TWO

Objectives
1. To complete the theme projects activity
2. To expose all students to a wide variety of information related to the themes in *Huckleberry Finn*
3. To give students the opportunity to practice making a presentation, public speaking, and having a leadership role

Activity
Allow one class period for each group's presentation. They can be done in any order you choose. In the unit outline for this unit they are set up as follows:

> Lesson Eighteen: Freedom
> Lesson Nineteen: Religion
> Lesson Twenty: Superstition
> Lesson Twenty-one: Education
> Lesson Twenty-two: Nature

These presentations are supposed to be complete, but since they have been done with relatively little teacher supervision, students may miss some important points. Make notes as you listen to the presentations, and at the end of the presentations (or if you find a convenient time during the presentations) be sure to go back and fill in any holes. ("Your presentation was great! I'm especially glad you brought out the points about _____. There are just a couple of things I'd like to add about the theme of _____." And proceed with your comments.)

An evaluation form is included with this unit for your convenience.

GROUP THEME PROJECT EVALUATION - *Huckleberry Finn*

Group Theme _____   Class _____

Group Members

_____   _____

_____   _____

_____   _____

Evaluation	Excellent	Good	Fair	Poor
Use of multi-media	4	3	2	1
Text Information	4	3	2	1
Real Life Information	4	3	2	1
Time Requirement	4	3	2	1
Enthusiasm	4	3	2	1
Organization	4	3	2	1
Could be seen/heard clearly	4	3	2	1
_____	4	3	2	1
_____	4	3	2	1

Total Points: _____   Grade _____

Comments:

LESSON TWENTY-THREE

Objectives
1. To summarize and review all the theme presentations
2. To give students the opportunity to practice writing to persuade
3. To give the teacher the opportunity to evaluate students' writing skills
4. To get students to think about and review the group presentations that were made

Activity #1

Take about one-half of this class period to review the theme presentations that your students have made. Make sure students jot down a few notes about each presentation so they will be able to complete Writing Assignment #3. For each group, review the theme that the group covered, the main points made about the theme in the text, and the main points made about the theme in real life. Fill in any gaps you found in the presentations, offering information as some additional ideas students may consider. Invite students' questions and comments.

Activity #2

Distribute Writing Assignment #3. Discuss the directions in detail and give students the remainder of the class period to work on it.

NOTE: In Writing Assignment #3 students will be persuading you which of the group presentations was the best. You might consider offering a prize of some sort to the group you are persuaded was the best or to the person/people who write the most persuasive essays.

WRITING ASSIGNMENT #3 - *Huckleberry Finn*

PROMPT
For the last week you have been bombarded with all kinds of information relating to the themes in *Huckleberry Finn*. Which group's presentation was the best? Your assignment is to persuade your teacher to agree with you which group had the best presentation.

PREWRITING
You have done part of your prewriting when you took notes in the review during the first part of this class period. Look back at your notes and briefly review each group's presentation once more. Which group do you think gave the best presentation? Give at least three good reasons why you think that group did the best. Next to those reasons, jot down a few examples of what you mean. What exactly in the presentation made you think of these reasons? You may also contrast this group's performance on these specific points with any other group's performance on the same points to help support your idea that the group you chose was the best.

DRAFTING
Write an introductory paragraph in which you set up the idea that the group presentation about _____ was the best.

In the body of your composition, write one paragraph (at least) for each of the reasons why you think this group did the best. Within the paragraph, use your specific examples to support your statements.

Write a concluding paragraph to summarize your ideas and close your composition.

PROMPT
When you finish the rough draft of your paper, ask a student who sits near you to read it. After reading your rough draft, he/she should tell you what he/she liked best about your work, which parts were difficult to understand, and ways in which your work could be improved. Reread your paper considering your critic's comments and make the corrections you think are necessary.

PROOFREADING
Do a final proofreading of your paper double-checking your grammar, spelling, organization, and the clarity of your ideas.

LESSON TWENTY-FOUR

Objective
To review the main ideas presented in *Huckleberry Finn*

Activity #1

Choose one of the review games/activities included in this unit and spend your class period as outlined there. Some materials for these activities are located in the Extra Activities section of this unit.

Activity #2

Remind students that the Unit Test will be in the next class meeting. Stress the review of the Study Guides and their class notes as a last-minute, brush-up review for homework.

REVIEW GAMES/ACTIVITIES - *Huckleberry Finn*

1. Ask the class to make up a unit test for *Huckleberry Finn*. The test should have 4 sections: matching, true/false, short answer, and essay. Students may use 1/2 period to make the test and then swap papers and use the other 1/2 class period to take a test a classmate has devised. (open book) You may want to use the unit test included in this packet or take questions from the students' unit tests to formulate your own test.

2. Take 1/2 period for students to make up true and false questions (including the answers). Collect the papers and divide the class into two teams. Draw a big tick-tack-toe board on the chalk board. Make one team X and one team O. Ask questions to each side, giving each student one turn. If the question is answered correctly, that students' team's letter (X or O) is placed in the box. If the answer is incorrect, no mark is placed in the box. The object is to get three marks in a row like tic-tac-toe. You may want to keep track of the number of games won for each team.

3. Take 1/2 period for students to make up questions (true/false and short answer). Collect the questions. Divide the class into two teams. You'll alternate asking questions to individual members of teams A & B (like in a spelling bee). The question keeps going from A to B until it is correctly answered, then a new question is asked. A correct answer does not allow the team to get another question. Correct answers are +2 points; incorrect answers are -1 point.

4. Have students pair up and quiz each other from their study guides and class notes.

5. Give students a *Huckleberry Finn* crossword puzzle to complete.

6. Divide your class into two teams. Use the *Huckleberry Finn* crossword words with their letters jumbled as a word list. Student 1 from Team A faces off against Student 1 from Team B. You write the first jumbled word on the board. The first student (1A or 1B) to unscramble the word wins the chance for his/her team to score points. If 1A wins the jumble, go to student 2A and give him/her a clue. He/she must give you the correct word which matches that clue. If he/she does, Team A scores a point, and you give student 3A a clue for which you expect another correct response. Continue giving Team A clues until some team member makes an incorrect response. An incorrect response sends the game back to the jumbled-word face off, this time with students 2A and 2B. Instead of repeating giving clues to the first few students of each team, continue with the student after the one who gave the last incorrect response on the team. For example, if Team B wins the jumbled-word face-off, and student 5B gave the last incorrect answer for Team B, you would start this round of clue questions with student 6B, and so on. The team with the most points wins!

LESSON TWENTY-FIVE

Objective
   To test the students' understanding of the main ideas and themes in *Huckleberry Finn*

Activity #1
   Distribute the unit tests. Go over the instructions in detail and allow the students the entire class period to complete the exam.

NOTES ABOUT THE UNIT TESTS IN THIS UNIT:
   There are 5 different unit tests which follow.
   There are two short answer tests which are based primarily on facts from the novel.
   There is one advanced short answer unit test. It is based on the extra discussion questions and quotations. Use the matching key for short answer unit test 2 to check the matching section of the advanced short answer unit test. There is no key for the short answer questions and quotations. The answers will be based on the discussions you have had during class.
   There are two multiple choice unit tests. Following the two unit tests, you will find an answer sheet on which students should mark their answers. The same answer sheet should be used for both tests; however, students' answers will be different for each test. Following the students' answer sheet for the multiple choice tests you will find your answer keys.
   The short answer tests have a vocabulary section. You should choose 10 of the vocabulary words from this unit, read them orally and have the students write them down. Then, either have students write a definition or use the words in sentences.

   Use these words for the vocabulary section of the advanced short answer unit test:

abolitionist	admirable	disposition	evade
impudent	lamented	feud	pensive
prejudiced	sanctified	speculate	tedious

Activity #2
   Collect all test papers and assigned books prior to the end of the class period.

UNIT TESTS

SHORT ANSWER UNIT TEST 1 - *Huckleberry Finn*

I. Matching/Identify

___ 1. Huck Finn   A. Man who invests Huck's money

___ 2. Tom Sawyer   B. Miss Watson's slave

___ 3. Widow Douglas   C. Huck's guardian

___ 4. Miss Watson   D. Narrator

___ 5. Jim   E. Feud with Shepherdsons

___ 6. Pap   F. Huck's friend who dreams

___ 7. Judge Thatcher   G. Huck's father

___ 8. Jim Turner   H. Frauds; cheaters

___ 9. The Grangerfords   I. Man who shoots Boggs

___ 10. Duke and King   J. Wealthy Englishman who died

___ 11. Boggs   K. Murderer on a sinking ship

___ 12. Col. Sherburn   L. Widow's sister

___ 13. Peter Wilks   M. Buys Jim for ransom

___ 14. Silas Phelps   N. Drunkard who is shot

___ 15. Aunt Sally   O. Tom's aunt

Huck Finn Short Answer Unit Test 1 Page 2

I. Short Answer

1. Identify Walter Scott.

2. Why does Pap yell at Huck for becoming civilized?

3. How did Huck "die"? Why?

4. Why is it important when Huck says, "All right, then, I'll go to hell!"?

5. Why does Huck assume Tom Sawyer's identity?

6. Why is Tom's plan to free Jim cruel?

7. How does Huck appear superior to Tom?

8. Why doesn't Huck's conscience bother him when he lies so much?

9. What is Twain's point about nature versus civilization?

10. Give at least three examples of superstition in *Huckleberry Finn*.

Huck Finn Short Answer Unit Test 1 Page 3

III. Composition

What is the point of *Huckleberry Finn*? When we read books, we usually come away from our reading experience a little richer, having given more thought to a particular aspect of life. What do you think Mark Twain intended us to gain from reading his novel?

Huck Finn Short Answer Unit Test 1 Page 4

IV. Vocabulary

    Listen to the vocabulary words and write them down. Go back later and fill in the correct definition for each word.

1.

2.

3.

4.

5.

6.

7.

8.

9.

10.

KEY: SHORT ANSWER UNIT TEST #1 - *Huckleberry Finn*

I. Matching/Identify

_D_	1. Huck Finn	A.	Man who invests Huck's money
_F_	2. Tom Sawyer	B.	Miss Watson's slave
_C_	3. Widow Douglas	C.	Huck's guardian
_L_	4. Miss Watson	D.	Narrator
_B_	5. Jim	E.	Feud with Shepherdsons
_G_	6. Pap	F.	Huck's friend who dreams
_A_	7. Judge Thatcher	G.	Huck's father
_K_	8. Jim Turner	H.	Frauds; cheaters
_E_	9. The Grangerfords	I.	Man who shoots Boggs
_H_	10. Duke and King	J.	Wealthy Englishman who died
_N_	11. Boggs	K.	Murderer on a sinking ship
_I_	12. Col. Sherburn	L.	Widow's sister
_J_	13. Peter Wilks	M.	Buys Jim for ransom
_M_	14. Silas Phelps	N.	Drunkard who is shot
_O_	15. Aunt Sally	O.	Tom's aunt

II. Short Answer

1. Identify Walter Scott.
    The Walter Scott was the wreck on which Huck found Jim Turner and his gang.

2. Why does Pap yell at Huck for becoming civilized?
    Huck's being educated and "civilized" makes Pap feel inferior. Since he's too lazy to improve himself, he yells at Huck.

3. How did Huck "die"? Why?
    Huck made it look like someone had broken into the cabin, murdered him, and dragged the body to the river. Being "dead," he wouldn't have to worry about Pap coming to find him or the Widow and Miss Watson "civilizing" him.

4. Why is it important when Huck says, "All right, then, I'll go to hell!"?
   It shows that Huck has thought about his relationship with Jim and has determined that he should help his friend out of slavery even though society says he would be wrong. He is prepared to take the consequences for his actions.

5. Why does Huck assume Tom Sawyer's identity?
   Mrs. Phelps mistakenly identifies him as Tom. He plays along with her so his true identity will not be known.

6. Why is Tom's plan to free Jim cruel?
   Jim could easily have been free much sooner than Tom's plan allowed. Also, some of the things Tom had Jim do, like living with spiders and snakes, were unpleasant.

7. How does Huck appear superior to Tom?
   Huck's common-sense plans seem far superior to Tom's childish adventure games he derived from books.

8. Why doesn't Huck's conscience bother him when he lies so much?
   He believes in the good cause for which he lies.

9. What is Twain's point about nature versus civilization?
   Nature has a good, revitalizing effect whereas civilization tends to bring out the worst in people.

10. Give at least three examples of superstition in *Huckleberry Finn*.
    Jim's talk about witches, the snakeskin bringing bad luck, the spider burning in the candle being bad luck. (There are many other acceptable examples.)

III. Written Paragraphs
   What is the point of *Huckleberry Finn*? When we read books, we usually come away from our reading experience a little richer, having given more thought to a particular aspect of life. What do you think Mark Twain intended us to gain from reading his novel?

IV. Vocabulary
   Choose ten of the vocabulary words. Read them orally to your class so the students can write them down on Part IV of their vocabulary terms.

SHORT ANSWER UNIT TEST 2 - *Huckleberry Finn*

I. Matching/Identify

____ 1. Huck Finn	A.	Huck's father
____ 2. Tom Sawyer	B.	Murderer on a sinking ship
____ 3. Widow Douglas	C.	Tom's aunt
____ 4. Miss Watson	D.	Frauds; cheaters
____ 5. Jim	E.	Buys Jim for ransom
____ 6. Pap	F.	Huck's friend who dreams
____ 7. Judge Thatcher	G.	Drunkard who is shot
____ 8. Jim Turner	H.	Narrator
____ 9. The Grangerfords	I.	Man who shoots Boggs
____ 10. Duke and King	J.	Wealthy Englishman who died
____ 11. Boggs	K.	Miss Watson's slave
____ 12. Col. Sherburn	L.	Huck's guardian
____ 13. Peter Wilks	M.	Feud with Shepherdsons
____ 14. Silas Phelps	N.	Man who invests Huck's money
____ 15. Aunt Sally	O.	Widow's sister

Huck Finn Short Answer Unit Test 2 Page 2

II. Short Answer

1. What does Huck think about religion -- specifically the good place, the bad place and prayer?

2. Contrast Huck and Tom. What are their main differences?

3. Why does Pap yell at Huck for becoming civilized? Is he right?

4. How do you know that material things don't matter to Huck?

5. What purpose(s) does Huck's death serve?

6. Compare/contrast Huck & Jim.

Huck Finn Short Answer Unit Test 2 Page 3

7. Explain the differences between Huck and the hunters.

8. Give two examples of the "cleverness" of the king and duke.

9. Why doesn't Huck's conscience bother him when he lies so much?

10. Why it is important that Huck says, "All right, then, I'll go to hell."?

Huck Finn Short Answer Unit Test 2 Page 4

III. Composition

    Mark Twain wrote *Huckleberry Finn* about a hundred years ago and here we are reading it so many years later. Why? What makes this book a classic?

IV. Vocabulary

    Listen to the vocabulary words and write them down. Go back later and fill in the correct definition for each word.

1.

2.

3.

4.

5.

6.

7.

8.

9.

10.

KEY: SHORT ANSWER UNIT TEST 2 *Huckleberry Finn*

I. Matching (Use this matching key also for the Advanced Short Answer Unit Test)

H	1. Huck Finn	A. Huck's father
F	2. Tom Sawyer	B. Murderer on a sinking ship
L	3. Widow Douglas	C. Tom's aunt
O	4. Miss Watson	D. Frauds; cheaters
K	5. Jim	E. Buys Jim for ransom
A	6. Pap	F. Huck's friend who dreams
N	7. Judge Thatcher	G. Drunkard who is shot
B	8. Jim Turner	H. Narrator
M	9. The Grangerfords	I. Man who shoots Boggs
D	10. Duke and King	J. Wealthy Englishman who died
G	11. Boggs	K. Miss Watson's slave
I	12. Col. Sherburn	L. Huck's guardian
J	13. Peter Wilks	M. Feud with Shepherdsons
E	14. Silas Phelps	N. Man who invests Huck's money
C	15. Aunt Sally	O. Widow's sister

II. Short Answer

1. What does Huck think about religion--specifically the good place, the bad place and prayer?
    Huck doesn't believe in formal religion. If the "good place" is going to be boring, he doesn't want to go there. If his friends go to the "bad place," that is where he wants to go. Huck "don't take no stock" in prayer since it doesn't seem to do him any immediate good.

2. Contrast Huck and Tom. What are their main differences?
    Huck is very practical and full of common sense. Tom is a dreamer and a bookworm, full of grand ideas which are for the most part impractical.

3. Why does Pap yell at Huck for becoming civilized? Is he right?

    Pap yells at Huck for becoming civilized because Huck's being civilized makes Pap feel inferior. Huck is becoming educated while Pap remains ignorant. Pap is not right to yell at Huck; he should have been proud of his son's accomplishments.

4. How do you know that material things don't matter to Huck?

    Huck is always leaving material things behind. He travels light and uses whatever he can find handy to suit his needs. Also, he gave all of his money to Judge Thatcher. Material things don't mean anything to him compared to his freedom.

5. What purpose(s) does Huck's death serve?

    Being "dead," Huck is truly free. He doesn't have to worry about Pap or Widow Douglas or Miss Watson coming to find him.

6. Compare/contrast Huck & Jim.

    Huck and Jim are both looking for freedom. Both have run away, and both have common sense. Both are superstitious, though Huck is a little less so than Jim. Jim is much older than Huck, almost a father-like figure, giving him advice and trying to keep him from harm.

7. Explain the differences between Huck and the hunters.

    The hunters were interested in collecting reward money. Huck wasn't interested in the money; he was trying to do the "right" thing. The hunters considered the runaway slaves as property; Huck considered Jim as a friend.

8. Give two examples of the "cleverness" of the king and duke.

    At the Pokeville camp meeting, the king got up and convinced the preacher to let him speak to the people. He told them that he was a pirate, now poor and reformed, who wanted to return to the Indian Ocean to reform other pirates. He asked for money for his cause, and the people gave him some.
    The duke printed up hand bills describing Jim as a runaway slave and offering a reward. He decided they would tie ropes around him to pretend they were "taking him in" so they could run the raft in the daytime.

9. Why doesn't Huck's conscience bother him when he lies so much?

    Huck's conscience doesn't bother him when he lies because he is lying for a good cause (or for what he thinks is the right cause).

10. Why it is important that Huck says, "All right, then, I'll go to hell."?

    Huck has thought about his relationship with Jim. He has decided that Jim is his friend, and that the right thing to do is to get him out of slavery again, regardless of the consequences.

ADVANCED SHORT ANSWER UNIT TEST - *Huckleberry Finn*

I. Matching

____ 1. Huck Finn   A. Huck's father

____ 2. Tom Sawyer   B. Murderer on a sinking ship

____ 3. Widow Douglas   C. Tom's aunt

____ 4. Miss Watson   D. Frauds; cheaters

____ 5. Jim   E. Buys Jim for ransom

____ 6. Pap   F. Huck's friend who dreams

____ 7. Judge Thatcher   G. Drunkard who is shot

____ 8. Jim Turner   H. Narrator

____ 9. The Grangerfords   I. Man who shoots Boggs

____ 10. Duke and King   J. Wealthy Englishman who died

____ 11. Boggs   K. Miss Watson's slave

____ 12. Col. Sherburn   L. Huck's guardian

____ 13. Peter Wilks   M. Feud with Shepherdsons

____ 14. Silas Phelps   N. Man who invests Huck's money

____ 15. Aunt Sally   O. Widow's sister

Huck Finn Advanced Short Answer Unit Test 2 Page 2
II. Short Answer
Interpretation
1. Explain why Mark Twain used Huck as the narrator and what effect it has on us as readers.

2. What are the main conflicts in the story? Are all the conflicts resolved? Explain how those that are resolved are resolved, and explain why those that are not resolved are not.

3. Does Huck develop or change as a result of his adventures? Explain how he does if he does, or why he does not if he does not.

4. What is *satire*? Give several examples of Twain's use of satire in *Huckleberry Finn*.

Huck Finn Advanced Short Answer Unit Test 2 Page 3

5. Discuss the importance of these characters in *Huckleberry Finn*. Why were they included in the story?

    Jim

    Pap

    King and Duke

    Grangerfords and Shepherdsons

    Tom

    Widow Douglas

    Jim Turner

Huck Finn Advanced Short Answer Unit Test 2 Page 4

III. Composition

You are Mark Twain. You are coming to this English/Language Arts class, which has read *Huckleberry Finn*, to explain how you used that novel to show your view of mankind. What will you say?

Huck Finn Advanced Short Answer Unit Test 2 Page 5

IV. Vocabulary

Listen to your vocabulary words and write them down. Go back later and write a composition in which you use all of the words. The composition should in some way relate to *Huckleberry Finn*.

MULTIPLE CHOICE UNIT TEST 1 - *Huckleberry Finn*

I. Matching/Identify

____ 1. Huck Finn	A. Man who invests Huck's money
____ 2. Tom Sawyer	B. Miss Watson's slave
____ 3. Widow Douglas	C. Huck's guardian
____ 4. Miss Watson	D. Narrator
____ 5. Jim	E. Feud with Shepherdsons
____ 6. Pap	F. Huck's friend who dreams
____ 7. Judge Thatcher	G. Huck's father
____ 8. Jim Turner	H. Frauds; cheaters
____ 9. The Grangerfords	I. Man who shoots Boggs
____ 10. Duke and King	J. Wealthy Englishman who died
____ 11. Boggs	K. Murderer on a sinking ship
____ 12. Col. Sherburn	L. Widow's sister
____ 13. Peter Wilks	M. Buys Jim for ransom
____ 14. Silas Phelps	N. Drunkard who is shot
____ 15. Aunt Sally	O. Tom's aunt

Huckleberry Finn Multiple Choice Unit Test 1 Page 2

I. Multiple Choice

1. Why doesn't Huck get along with Miss Watson and Widow Douglas?
    a. Huck doesn't get along with *anyone*.
    b. They want to civilize him and he wants to remain free.
    c. Huck's friends tell him to give the widow a hard time.
    d. Huck would rather live with Pap.

2. What does Huck think about religion--specifically the good place, the bad place and prayer?
    a. He wants to go to the "good place" and stay away from the "bad place" but he doesn't believe in prayer.
    b. He wants to go to the "bad place" and stay away from the "good place" and he prays often.
    c. He wants to go to the "bad place" because the "good place" would be boring but he prays often.
    d. He wants to go to the "bad place" because the "good place" would be boring. He doesn't believe in prayer.

3. What are the main differences between Huck and Tom?
    a. Huck is practical; Tom is a dreamer.
    b. Tom is superstitious; Huck is religious.
    c. Huck is smart; Tom is not very bright.
    d. Tom is dependable; Huck is not.

4. Why does Pap yell at Huck for becoming civilized?
    a. Pap feels inferior to his own son, so he yells at him.
    b. Huck is "putting on airs" and flaunting his knowledge just to embarrass Pap.
    c. Pap doesn't really yell at Huck; it's just his way of complimenting Huck.
    d. Pap is just trying to teach Huck a valuable lesson.

5. How do you know that material things don't matter to Huck?
    a. He is always leaving material things behind.
    b. He travels light and uses whatever he can find to suit his needs.
    c. He gave his money to Judge Thatcher.
    d. All of the above

6. What purpose(s) does Huck's death serve?
    a. Huck "gets even" with Widow Douglas because she was so mean to him.
    b. It throws Jim and Pap together so they must depend on each other.
    c. It gives him total freedom.
    d. It shows Huck how totally dependent on civilization he has become.

Huckleberry Finn Multiple Choice Unit Test 1 Page 3

7. Why do Huck and Jim begin their journey down the Mississippi?
    a. They've both always wanted to travel on the Mississippi.
    b. People began looking for them on Jackson's Island.
    c. A storm forces them off of the island.
    d. They just get tired of living on the island and decide to move on.

8. Why does Huck want to save Jim Turner?
    a. Huck began to think how dreadful it was, even for murderers to be in such a fix.
    b. Jim is his friend.
    c. Jim has information Huck needs.
    d. b & c

9. Why don't the slave hunters get Jim?
    a. Huck and Jim out-ran them.
    b. Jim was too ill to go with them.
    c. The hunters get tired of waiting and left.
    d. The hunters were afraid they would catch the disease Huck's father had.

10. Explain the differences between Huck and the hunters.
    a. The hunters wanted money; Huck wanted to do the right thing.
    b. The hunters considered Jim as property; Huck considered Jim a friend.
    c. The hunter's had Jim's best interest in mind; Huck didn't want to lose his travelling companion.
    d. a & b

11. Why did Twain include this adventure with the Grangerfords?
    a. Twain shows the foolish side of human nature.
    b. Twain shows Huck's determination to set Jim free.
    c. Twain shows the Grangerfords as a model family.
    d. Twain shows the Shepherdsons as a model family.

12. What's the point of the incident of the shooting of Boggs?
    a. It shows that there are heroes in everyday life.
    b. It shows the best of human nature.
    c. It points out many weaknesses in human character.
    d. It furthers the subplot of Jim's quest for freedom.

Huckleberry Finn Multiple Choice Unit Test 1 Page 4

13. Why doesn't Huck's conscience bother him when he lies so much?
    a. His conscience never bothers him.
    b. He is lying for a good cause.
    c. He just doesn't think about it.
    d. a & c

14. Why it is important that Huck says, "All right, then, I'll go to hell."?
    a. He has turned his back on the religion which has so often helped him.
    b. He has chosen what is right according to his conscience rather than according to social or religious rules.
    c. He has become such good friends with Jim that he would risk the eternal happiness of his soul to do what he thinks is right for his friend.
    d. b & c

15. Why does Huck assume Tom Sawyer's identity?
    a. He admires Tom and since he can't be himself, he chooses to be Tom.
    b. Mrs. Phelps mistakes him for Tom, so he plays along.
    c. He wants to be able to "think like Tom" so he will know what to do in every situation.
    d. He just decides to do it as he is walking down the road. He'd been thinking about Tom and it seemed like a good idea.

16. What's the difference between Tom's plan for freeing Jim and Huck's?
    a. Tom's is practical; Huck's is unrealistic.
    b. Tom's takes less time.
    c. Huck's is practical; Tom's is unrealistic.
    d. Huck's is harder on Jim.

17. Tom's plan is actually cruel. Why?
    a. Jim could be free and not worrying about his situation while he is going through the ridiculous rites Tom thinks are necessary.
    b. The rites Tom thinks up are not very pleasant for Jim
    c. a & b
    d. None of the above

Huckleberry Finn Multiple Choice Unit Test 1 Page 5

III. Composition

    Explain how Twain uses humor, satire, and his characters to make his points to the reader about religion, education, and freedom.

Huckleberry Finn Multiple Choice Unit Test 1 Page 6

IV. Vocabulary

___ 1. COUNTERFEIT   A. persistently persuading
___ 2. ADMIRABLE   B. a woman's dress
___ 3. SULTRY   C. hypnotism
___ 4. BYGONES   D. tiresome by reason of length; boring
___ 5. MESMERISM   E. to cut off
___ 6. HUFFY   F. very humid and hot
___ 7. VICTUALS   G. a preconceived preference
___ 8. BERTH   H. a hereditary fight
___ 9. SANCTIFIED   I. gloomy; depressing
___10. RASPY   J. a place to sleep
___11. ABREAST   K. make a risky financial transaction
___12. AMPUTATE   L. holy; inviolable
___13. TEDIOUS   M. food
___14. FROCK   N. a fit of anger or annoyance
___15. PREJUDICE   O. past happenings
___16. FEUD   P. side by side
___17. SPECULATE   Q. grieving
___18. DISMAL   R. deserving admiration
___19. LAMENTED   S. fake; not real
___20. COAXING   T. grating, harsh

MULTIPLE CHOICE UNIT TEST 2 - *Huckleberry Finn*

I. Matching

____ 1. Huck Finn   A. Huck's father

____ 2. Tom Sawyer   B. Murderer on a sinking ship

____ 3. Widow Douglas   C. Tom's aunt

____ 4. Miss Watson   D. Frauds; cheaters

____ 5. Jim   E. Buys Jim for ransom

____ 6. Pap   F. Huck's friend who dreams

____ 7. Judge Thatcher   G. Drunkard who is shot

____ 8. Jim Turner   H. Narrator

____ 9. The Grangerfords I. Man who shoots Boggs

____ 10. Duke and King   J. Wealthy Englishman who died

____ 11. Boggs   K. Miss Watson's slave

____ 12. Col. Sherburn   L. Huck's guardian

____ 13. Peter Wilks   M. Feud with Shepherdsons

____ 14. Silas Phelps   N. Man who invests Huck's money

____ 15. Aunt Sally   O. Widow's sister

Huckleberry Finn Multiple Choice Unit Test 2 Page 2

II. Multiple Choice

1. Why doesn't Huck get along with Miss Watson and Widow Douglas?
    a. Huck doesn't get along with *anyone*.
    b. Huck would rather live with Pap.
    c. Huck's friends tell him to give the widow a hard time.
    d. They want to civilize him and he wants to remain free.

2. What does Huck think about religion -- specifically the good place, the bad place and prayer?
    a. He wants to go to the "bad place" because the "good place" would be boring. He doesn't believe in prayer.
    b. He wants to go to the "bad place" and stay away from the "good place" and he prays often.
    c. He wants to go to the "bad place" because the "good place" would be boring but he prays often.
    d. He wants to go to the "good place" and stay away from the "bad place" but he doesn't believe in prayer.

3. What are the main differences between Huck and Tom?
    a. Huck is smart; Tom is not very bright.
    b. Tom is superstitious; Huck is religious.
    c. Huck is practical; Tom is a dreamer.
    d. Tom is dependable; Huck is not.

4. Why does Pap yell at Huck for becoming civilized?
    a. Pap is just trying to teach Huck a valuable lesson.
    b. Huck is "putting on airs" and flaunting his knowledge just to embarrass Pap.
    c. Pap doesn't really yell at Huck; it's just his way of complimenting Huck.
    d. Pap feels inferior to his own son so he yells at him.

5. How do you know that material things don't matter to Huck?
    a. He is always leaving material things behind.
    b. He travels light and uses whatever he can find to suit his needs.
    c. He gave his money to Judge Thatcher.
    d. All of the above

6. What purpose(s) does Huck's death serve?
    a. Huck "gets even" with Widow Douglas because she was so mean to him.
    b. It gives him total freedom.
    c. It throws Jim and Pap together so they must depend on each other.
    d. It shows Huck how totally dependent on civilization he has become.

Huckleberry Finn Multiple Choice Unit Test 2 Page 3

7. Why do Huck and Jim begin their journey down the Mississippi?
    a. They've both always wanted to travel on the Mississippi.
    b. A storm forces them off of the island.
    c. People began looking for them on Jackson's Island.
    d. They just get tired of living on the island and decide to move on.

8. Why does Huck want to save Jim Turner?
    a. Jim has information Huck needs.
    b. Jim is his friend.
    c. Huck began to think how dreadful it was, even for murderers to be in such a fix.
    d. b & c

9. Why don't the slave hunters get Jim?
    a. The hunters were afraid they would catch the disease Huck's father had.
    b. Jim was too ill to go with them.
    c. The hunters get tired of waiting and left.
    d. Jim has information Huck needs.

10. Explain the differences between Huck and the hunters.
    a. The hunters wanted money; Huck wanted to help Miss Watson get Jim back.
    b. The hunters considered Jim as property; Huck considered Jim a friend.
    c. The hunter's had Jim's best interest in mind; Huck didn't want to lose his travelling companion.
    d. a & b

11. Why did Twain include this adventure with the Grangerfords?
    a. Twain shows Huck's determination to set Jim free.
    b. Twain shows the foolish side of human nature.
    c. Twain shows the Grangerfords as a model family.
    d. Twain contrasts the Grangerfords and Shepherdsons to show how families ought to be.

12. What's the point of the incident of the shooting of Boggs?
    a. It points out many weaknesses in human character.
    b. It shows the best of human nature.
    c. It shows that there are heroes in everyday life.
    d. It furthers the subplot of Jim's quest for freedom.

Huckleberry Finn Multiple Choice Unit Test 2 Page 4

13. Why doesn't Huck's conscience bother him when he lies so much?
    a. His conscience never bothers him.
    b. He doesn't have a conscience.
    c. He just doesn't think about it.
    d. He is lying for a good cause.

14. Why it is important that Huck says, "All right, then, I'll go to hell."?
    a. He has turned his back on the religion which has so often helped him.
    b. He has chosen what is right according to social rules instead of religious rules.
    c. He has become such good friends with Jim that he would risk the eternal happiness of his soul to do what he thinks is right for his friend.
    d. b & c

15. Why does Huck assume Tom Sawyer's identity?
    a. He admires Tom and since he can't be himself, he chooses to be Tom.
    b. He wants to be able to "think like Tom" so he will know what to do in every situation.
    c. Mrs. Phelps mistakes him for Tom, so he plays along with the situation.
    d. He just decides to do it as he is walking down the road. He'd been thinking about Tom and it seemed like a good idea.

16. What's the difference between Tom's plan for freeing Jim and Huck's?
    a. Tom's is practical; Huck's is unrealistic.
    b. Tom's takes less time.
    c. Huck's is harder on Jim.
    d. Huck's is practical; Tom's is unrealistic.

17. Tom's plan is actually cruel. Why?
    a. It makes Jim think he is free when, in fact, he is not.
    b. Jim could be free and not worrying about his situation while he is going through the ridiculous rites Tom thinks are necessary.
    c. a & b
    d. none of the above

Huckleberry Finn Multiple Choice Unit Test 2 Page 5

III. Composition

    Explain how Twain uses humor, satire, and his characters to make his points to the reader about religion, education, and freedom.

Huckleberry Finn Multiple Choice Unit Test 2 Page 6

IV. Vocabulary

___ 1. QUICKSILVER		A. holy; inviolable
___ 2. COUNTERFEIT		B. moderation, sobriety
___ 3. TEDIOUS		C. person against slavery
___ 4. ABREAST		D. past happenings
___ 5. INSURRECTION		E. pulled in conflicting emotional directions
___ 6. SANCTIFIED		F. excellent, having a sense of grandeur
___ 7. PETRIFIED		G. sad
___ 8. SUBLIME		H. post of timber or iron for support
___ 9. ABOLITIONIST		I. mercury
___ 10. STANCHION		J. tiresome by reason of length; boring
___ 11. DISTRACTED		K. to obtain by persistent persuasion
___ 12. WARBLING		L. turned to stone
___ 13. MOURNFUL		M. to escape or avoid by cleverness or deceit
___ 14. EVADE		N. side by side
___ 15. TEMPERANCE		O. the act or an instance of open revolt
___ 16. FEUD		P. a hereditary fight
___ 17. PHRENOLOGY		Q. reading a person's future by examining their skull
___ 18. CONVENIENCES		R. singing
___ 19. COAXING		S. false; fake
___ 20. BYGONES		T. things that increase comfort or save work

ANSWER SHEET - *Huckleberry Finn*
Multiple Choice Unit Tests

Place your answers to the test questions on this page. Part III may be answered on the back of this page or on a separate sheet of notebook paper.

I. Matching	II. Multiple Choice	IV. Vocabulary
1. ___	1. ___	1. ___
2. ___	2. ___	2. ___
3. ___	3. ___	3. ___
4. ___	4. ___	4. ___
5. ___	5. ___	5. ___
6. ___	6. ___	6. ___
7. ___	7. ___	7. ___
8. ___	8. ___	8. ___
9. ___	9. ___	9. ___
10. ___	10. ___	10. ___
11. ___	11. ___	11. ___
12. ___	12. ___	12. ___
13. ___	13. ___	13. ___
14. ___	14. ___	14. ___
15. ___	15. ___	15. ___
	16. ___	16. ___
	17. ___	17. ___
		18. ___
		19. ___
		20. ___

ANSWER KEY - *Huckleberry Finn*
Multiple Choice Unit Tests

I. Matching
1. D   H
2. F   F
3. C   L
4. L   O
5. B   K
6. G   A
7. A   N
8. K   B
9. E   M
10. H D
11. N G
12. I I
13. J J
14. M E
15. O C

II. Multiple Choice
1. B   D
2. D   A
3. A   C
4. A   D
5. D   D
6. C   B
7. B   C
8. A   C
9. D   A
10. C B
11. A B
12. C A
13. B D
14. D C
15. B C
16. C D
17. C B

IV. Vocabulary
1. S   I
2. R   S
3. F   J
4. O   N
5. C   O
6. N   A
7. M   L
8. J   F
9. L   C
10. T H
11. P E
12. E R
13. D G
14. B M
15. G B
16. H P
17. K Q
18. I T
19. Q K
20. A D

UNIT RESOURCE MATERIALS

BULLETIN BOARD IDEAS - *Huckleberry Finn*

1. Save one corner of the board for the best of students' *Huckleberry Finn* writing assignments.

2. Take one of the word search puzzles from the extra activities section, and with a marker copy it over in a large size on the bulletin board. Write the clue words to find to one side. Invite students prior to and after class to find the words and circle them on the bulletin board.

3. Write several of the most significant quotations from the book onto the board on brightly colored paper.

4. Make a bulletin board listing the vocabulary words for this unit. As you complete sections of the novel and discuss the vocabulary for each section, write the definitions on the bulletin board. (If your board is one students face frequently, it will help them learn the words.)

5. Make a cut-out Huck Finn fishing in the river with each of the novel's themes on a cut-out fish in the river.

6. Put up a large map of the U.S. Highlight the Mississippi River an put a big cut-out star at Hannibal. Cut out letters: "HUCKLEBERRY FINN: AN AMERICAN NOVEL" for above the map. Cut out letters for each of the themes and put them around the outside of the map in the empty space left on the board.

7. Divide your board into five sections, one for each of the themes (freedom/bondage, education, nature, superstition, and religion). Post information/articles/pictures relating to the themes in our world today in the appropriate sections.

8. Write the grammar worksheet up on the bulletin board. Leave room to write a corrected version next to it. After individual students do the worksheet, use your bulletin board to discuss the corrections with your students and to write a corrected version of the passage.

9. Make a general HOTLINE bulletin board with phone numbers and related information where people can call for help for child abuse, runaways, alcohol and drug abuse, and homelessness. (All of these also relate to *Huck Finn*, if you stop and think about it for a minute.)

10. Do a bulletin board about your students' pastimes. What do they do when they are home alone or without parental supervision? Have students make contributions to this board.

11. Make a bulletin board about education--especially higher education if you are teaching juniors or seniors. What are a student's options, what decisions have to be made, where can one get information, etc.

EXTRA ACTIVITIES - *Huck Finn*

One of the difficulties in teaching a novel is that all students don't read at the same speed. One student who likes to read may take the book home and finish it in a day or two. Sometimes a few students finish the in-class assignments early. The problem, then, is finding suitable extra activities for students.

The best thing I've found is to keep a little library in the classroom. For this unit on *Huckleberry Finn*, you might check out from the school library other books and stories by Mark Twain, especially his humorous short sketches. You could include other related books and articles about the Mississippi River, river boats, slavery, foster homes, history of the period, etc. Information about islands, parks and other natural resources would also be appropriate.

Other things you may keep on hand are puzzles. We have made some relating directly to *Huckleberry Finn* for you. Feel free to duplicate them.

Some students may like to draw. You might devise a contest or allow some extra-credit grade for students who draw characters or scenes from *Huckleberry Finn*. Note, too, that if the students do not want to keep their drawings you may pick up some extra bulletin board materials this way. If you have a contest and you supply the prize (a CD or something like that perhaps), you could, possibly, make the drawing itself a non-refundable entry fee.

The pages which follow contain games, puzzles and worksheets. The keys, when appropriate, immediately follow the puzzle or worksheet. There are two main groups of activities: one group for the unit; that is, generally relating to the *Huckleberry Finn* text, and another group of activities related strictly to the *Huckleberry Finn* vocabulary.

Directions for these games, puzzles and worksheets are self-explanatory. The object here is to provide you with extra materials you may use in any way you choose.

MORE ACTIVITIES - *Huckleberry Finn*

1. Pick a chapter or scene with a great deal of dialogue and have the students act it out on a stage. (Perhaps you could assign various scenes to different groups of students so more than one scene could be acted and more students could participate.)

2. Have students work together to make a time line chronology of the events in the story. Take a large piece of construction paper and on one wall (or however you can physically arrange it in your room) create a "river" and make the events of the story along it. Students may want to add drawings or cut-out pictures to represent the events (as well as a written statement).

3. Show the film *Huckleberry Finn* after you have completed reading the novel in class. Have students evaluate the movie and compare/contrast it with the book. If the students have tried writing a chapter into a scene in a play, you may wish to discuss how the problems they encountered in changing the form were handled in the movie.

4. Have students design a book cover (front and back and inside flaps) for *Huckleberry Finn*.

5. Have students design a bulletin board (ready to be put up; not just sketched) for *Huckleberry Finn*.

6. Have students group the chapters together to show the larger structure of the novel. Have them explain why they chose the divisions they made.

7. Have students choose one chapter of the book (with sufficient dialogue) to rewrite as a play. In conjunction with this assignment, have students write a composition explaining the difficulties they encountered in changing from one written form to another.

8. Have a Mississippi River Day during which you explore the history, commerce, and importance of the Mississippi River. You might do a little study of the states through which the river runs.

9. Have students write a composition in which they tell what they would do if they were as free as Huck.

10. Do a study of the natural areas left in our country--parks, wildlife preservations, etc.

11. See bulletin board ideas #s 10, 11, & 12. A whole lesson or even a mini-unit could be centered around any of the ideas set forth there.

WORD SEARCH - *Huckleberry Finn*

All words in this list are associated with *Huckleberry Finn*. The words are placed backwards, forward, diagonally, up and down. The included words are listed below the word searches.

```
H A N N I B A L X P S T H A T C H E R P P T B H
P W B K A S X R Q Y S F R Q I M R X H K B F H H
L F H W Z T B H F B Z R R V D M Y T P N G Q Y L
L V S F H V U C R Y X T I M Q N T C R S J A J P
S J W T G I K R A P X L Z Y K F T C O F F I N W
D B D V Z S S B E B I D M C E G I B V R L I V G
P R G R J T V K K Z I T D I P N O S R W A O G C
B O G G S L A V E K A N S H S A R A H W J I M P
H S L E P T N D X Y A L O K Y S F A T I I G R G
L R S L M N A O P L W B L I P T I C H H N D P R
T O M E Y I N O S V F I U A T T S S L W L G O F
M F F N N E S I B T W R P C B A U A S E D U F W
N N K T P R L S F R A A E K K R C R L I M B C M
C P G A U A A Y O K E W L E T X I U N L P E M K
L B C H S S X H H U C V W T D R B A D E Y P N T
Q S X Q W W S W P G R U I P E O F K H E R Y I S
E R E L I G I O N J Q I H R L R M A T T R E S S
```

BOGGS	HANNIBAL	MISSOURI	SLAVE
BUCK	HARNESS	MOSES	SNAKE
CABIN	HARNEY	NATURE	THATCHER
CIVILIZED	HOG	OATH	TOM
CLEMENS	HUCK FINN	PAP	TURNER
COFFIN	ISLAND	POLLY	TWAIN
EDUCATION	JIM	RAFT	WALTER
ESCAPE	LOFTUS	RELIGION	WATSON
FISHING	LUCK	RIVERBOATS	WHISKEY
FREEDOM	MATTRESS	SALLY	WIDOW
GANG	MISSISSIPPI	SARAH	WILKS
HAIRBALL		SILAS	

KEY: WORD SEARCH - *Huckleberry Finn*

All words in this list are associated with *Huckleberry Finn*. The words are placed backwards, forward, diagonally, up and down. The included words are listed below the word searches.

```
         H A N N I B A L           T H A T C H E R
                 A                         I
             W T                   V               G
             H   U C           I                       A
             I     R A     L Y   F   C O F F I N
                 S   E B I   M E   I       L I   G
        P G       K   Z I   D   N O S R   A O
        B O G G S L A V E K A N S   S A R A H W J I M
        H S L E   T N D   Y A L O K   S F A T I I     G
        L   S L M N A O   L   B L I P T I C H H N D
        T O M E Y I N O S   F I U A T T S S L   L G O
        M   F   N E S I B T W R P C B A U A S E   U   W
                T P R L S F R A A E   K R C R L I M   C
                  A U A A   O K E W L E     I U N L P E   K
                  C   S S   H   U C V   T D     A D E Y P N
              S                 R U I   E O       H E R   I S
              E R E L I G I O N   I H R   R M A T T R E S S
```

BOGGS	HANNIBAL	MISSOURI	SLAVE
BUCK	HARNESS	MOSES	SNAKE
CABIN	HARNEY	NATURE	THATCHER
CIVILIZED	HOG	OATH	TOM
CLEMENS	HUCK FINN	PAP	TURNER
COFFIN	ISLAND	POLLY	TWAIN
EDUCATION	JIM	RAFT	WALTER
ESCAPE	LOFTUS	RELIGION	WATSON
FISHING	LUCK	RIVERBOATS	WHISKEY
FREEDOM	MATTRESS	SALLY	WIDOW
GANG	MISSISSIPPI	SARAH	WILKS
HAIRBALL		SILAS	

CROSSWORD - *Huckleberry Finn*

CROSSWORD CLUES - *Huckleberry Finn*

ACROSS
1. AKA Twain
6. A 'meow' was Tom's secret --- to Huck
8. Huck's hook and line pastime
10. The judge
13. Huck hides money there
14. Place in the house; bed----, living---, etc.
15. Col. Sherburn shot him
17. Sister to Widow Douglas
19. Novel; reading material
20. Mr. Finn to Huck
21. Solomon, for example
22. Opposite of short
23. Huck uses the blood of one to stage his own death
24. Past tense of 'eat'
26. It can be bad or good; fate
27. Place to sleep
28. Huck's girl name
30. Packard & Bill plot to kill him
35. Huck's river transportation
37. Marital status of the Douglas woman
38. Widow Douglas thinks Huck should get this at school
39. One bit Jim
40. Mr. Phelps
42. Opposite of come
43. Pledge
45. Jim's relationship to Miss Watson
47. Tom's aunt/guardian
48. River on which Huck and Jim traveled

DOWN
1. Huck and Jim find a dead man in one
2. King & Duke hide money there
3. Tom and Huck help Jim do this
4. He told Huck many superstitions
5. I discover _____ and the Bulrushers
7. Huck visits her in town, dressed as a girl
8. Opposite of slavery
9. Tom Sawyer was the leader of a _____ of boys
11. Huck's dreamer friend
12. The _____ Oracle
13. Conforming to rules of society
15. Grangerford boy Huck's age
16. Feud with Shepherdsons
17. _____ Scott
18. Theme relating to the outdoors
23. Twain's Hometown
25. Jackson's
29. Leads the mob against Col. Sherburn
30. Author Mark
31. Widow Douglas thinks Huck should get this at church
32. Narrator
33. Buck shot at this Shepherdson
34. Hannibal's state
36. Definite article
40. Mrs. Phelps; Tom's aunt
41. Questioned
44. Opposite of that
46. He

CROSSWORD ANSWER KEY - *Huckleberry Finn*

					C	L	E	M	E	N	S				E		J			M
C	A	L	L		A			A						F	I	S	H	I	N	G	O
			O		B		T	H	A	T	C	H	E	R		C		M		A	S
	C	O	F	F	I	N		T		O		A	E	A		A			N		E
	I		T		N		R	O	O	M		I		E		P		B	O	G	G	S
	V		U				E					R		D		E		U			R
	I		S		W	A	T	S	O	N		B	O	O	K		C		P	A	P
	L				A		S		A			A		M			K			N	
K	I	N	G		L				T	A	L	L						H	O	G	
	Z			A	T	E		I		U		L	U	C	K			A		E	
B	E	D			E		S	A	R	A	H				T	U	R	N	E	R	
	D				R		L		E		A				W		N		F		
R		H		H		M		A		R	A	F	T		A		W	I	D	O	W
E	D	U	C	A	T	I	O	N		K			H		I		B		R		
L		C		R		S		D		S	N	A	K	E		N		A		D	
I		K		N		S				E					S	I	L	A	S		
G	O			E		O	A	T	H		S	L	A	V	E		A		S		
I		H		Y		U		H			S						L		K		
O		I				R		I					P	O	L	L	Y		E		
N		M	I	S	S	I	S	S	I	P	P	I				Y		D			

MATCHING QUIZ/WORKSHEET 1 - *Huckleberry Finn*

___ 1. OATH   A. Tom Sawyer was the leader of a _____ of boys

___ 2. ESCAPE   B. Feud with Shepherdsons

___ 3. WATSON   C. Huck uses the blood of one to stage his own death

___ 4. POLLY   D. Widow Douglas thinks Huck should get this at church

___ 5. COFFIN   E. Mr. Finn to Huck

___ 6. THATCHER   F. _____ Scott

___ 7. HARNEY   G. Tom and Huck help Jim do this

___ 8. MISSISSIPPI   H. The judge

___ 9. RELIGION   I. Sister to Widow Douglas

___10. WALTER   J. Jackson's

___11. FISHING   K. Pledge

___12. ISLAND   L. Tom's aunt/guardian

___13. RAFT   M. Huck and Jim find a dead man in one

___14. HOG   N. Buck shot at this Shepherdson

___15. PAP   O. Huck's river transportation

___16. SARAH   P. Huck hides money there

___17. FREEDOM   Q. Opposite of slavery

___18. GRANGERFORDS R. River on which Huck and Jim traveled

___19. CABIN   S. Huck's girl name

___20. GANG   T. Huck's hook and line pastime

KEY: MATCHING QUIZ/WORKSHEET 1 - *Huckleberry Finn*

K 1. OATH   A. Tom Sawyer was the leader of a _____ of boys

G 2. ESCAPE   B. Feud with Shepherdsons

I 3. WATSON   C. Huck uses the blood of one to stage his own death

L 4. POLLY   D. Widow Douglas thinks Huck should get this at church

P 5. COFFIN   E. Mr. Finn to Huck

H 6. THATCHER   F. _____ Scott

N 7. HARNEY   G. Tom and Huck help Jim do this

R 8. MISSISSIPPI   H. The judge

D 9. RELIGION   I. Sister to Widow Douglas

F 10. WALTER   J. Jackson's

T 11. FISHING   K. Pledge

J 12. ISLAND   L. Tom's aunt/guardian

O 13. RAFT   M. Huck and Jim find a dead man in one

C 14. HOG   N. Buck shot at this Shepherdson

E 15. PAP   O. Huck's river transportation

S 16. SARAH   P. Huck hides money there

Q 17. FREEDOM   Q. Opposite of slavery

B 18. GRANGERFORDS R. River on which Huck and Jim traveled

M 19. CABIN   S. Huck's girl name

A 20. GANG   T. Huck's hook and line pastime

ATCHING QUIZ/WORKSHEET 2 - *Huckleberry Finn*

___ 1. THATCHER   A. Leads the mob against Col. Sherburn

___ 2. WALTER   B. Author Mark

___ 3. FREEDOM   C. Opposite of slavery

___ 4. KING   D. _____ Scott

___ 5. HARKNESS   E. Solomon, for example

___ 6. EDUCATION   F. Tom and Huck help Jim do this

___ 7. SALLY   G. Marital status of the Douglas woman

___ 8. MISSISSIPPI   H. Mrs. Phelps; Tom's aunt

___ 9. ISLAND   I. The judge

___ 10. ESCAPE   J. Buck shot at this Shepherdson

___ 11. GANG   K. Huck hides money there

___ 12. PAP   L. Widow Douglas thinks Huck should get this at school

___ 13. MOSES   M. River on which Huck and Jim traveled

___ 14. MATTRESS   N. Mr. Finn to Huck

___ 15. TWAIN   O. Huck's girl name

___ 16. SARAH   P. Huck uses the blood of one to stage his own death

___ 17. COFFIN   Q. Jackson's

___ 18. HARNEY   R. King & Duke hide money there

___ 19. HOG   S. I discover _____ and the Bulrushers

___ 20. WIDOW   T. Tom Sawyer was the leader of a _____ of boys

KEY: MATCHING QUIZ/WORKSHEET 2 - *Huckleberry Finn*

_I_	1. THATCHER	A. Leads the mob against Col. Sherburn
_D_	2. WALTER	B. Author Mark
_C_	3. FREEDOM	C. Opposite of slavery
_E_	4. KING	D. _____ Scott
_A_	5. HARKNESS	E. Solomon, for example
_L_	6. EDUCATION	F. Tom and Huck help Jim do this
_H_	7. SALLY	G. Marital status of the Douglas woman
_M_	8. MISSISSIPPI	H. Mrs. Phelps; Tom's aunt
_Q_	9. ISLAND	I. The judge
_F_	10. ESCAPE	J. Buck shot at this Shepherdson
_T_	11. GANG	K. Huck hides money there
_N_	12. PAP	L. Widow Douglas thinks Huck should get this at school
_S_	13. MOSES	M. River on which Huck and Jim traveled
_R_	14. MATTRESS	N. Mr. Finn to Huck
_B_	15. TWAIN	O. Huck's girl name
_O_	16. SARAH	P. Huck uses the blood of one to stage his own death
_K_	17. COFFIN	Q. Jackson's
_J_	18. HARNEY	R. King & Duke hide money there
_P_	19. HOG	S. I discover _____ and the Bulrushers
_G_	20. WIDOW	T. Tom Sawyer was the leader of a _____ of boys

JUGGLE LETTER REVIEW GAME CLUE SHEET - *Huckleberry Finn*

SCRAMBLED	WORD	CLUE
SESMO	MOSES	I discover _____ and the Bulrushers
GHO	HOG	Huck uses the blood of one to stage his own death
MCENSLE	CLEMENS	AKA Twain
KYHIWSE	WHISKEY	Pap's drink
THAO	OATH	Pledge
GSBOG	BOGGS	Col. Sherburn shot him
ISKLW	WILKS	Dead Peter
MTO	TOM	Huck's dreamer friend
REOFMDE	FREEDOM	Opposite of slavery
ATINW	TWAIN	Author Mark
SKRHENSA	HARKNESS	Leads the mob against Col. Sherburn
ANETUR	NATURE	Theme relating to the outdoors
APSEEC	ESCAPE	Tom and Huck help Jim do this
DOWWI	WIDOW	Marital status of the Douglas woman
KCUB	BUCK	Grangerford boy Huck's age
UNHCKNIF	HUCK FINN	Narrator
RTEWAL	WALTER	_____ Scott
RTTHHEAC	THATCHER	The judge
CKLU	LUCK	It can be bad or good; fate
DEFORRNRGASG	GRANGERFORDS	Feud with Shepherdsons
ESKAN	SNAKE	One bit Jim
SPPSISIIISM	MISSISSIPPI	River on which and Jim traveled
NGGA	GANG	Tom Sawyers was the leader of a _____.
IAAHRLLB	HAIRBALL	The _____ Oracle
ALABNIHN	HANNIBAL	Twain's hometown
RHYANE	HARNEY	Buck shot at this Shepherdson
ELZIDIVIC	CIVILIZED	Conforming to rules of society
INERIGLO	RELIGION	Widow Douglas thinks Huck should get this at church
TWANSO	WATSON	Sister to Widow Douglas
LYLPO	POLLY	Tom's aunt/guardian
MJI	JIM	He told Huck many superstitions
NADLSI	ISLAND	Jackson's
ESLAV	SLAVE	Jim's relationship to Miss Watson
CINDEOAUT	EDUCATION	Widow Douglas thinks Huck should get this at school
PPA	PAP	Mr. Finn to Huck
BCINA	CABIN	Huck and Jim find a dead man in one
AFTR	RAFT	Huck's river transportation

VOCABULARY RESOURCE MATERIALS

VOCABULARY WORD SEARCH - *Huckleberry Finn*

All words in this list are associated with *Huckleberry Finn* with an emphasis on the vocabulary words chosen for study in the text. The words are placed backwards, forward, diagonally, up and down. The included words are listed below.

```
T W S N S L A D X P K N X Z D H B Q N H R X F G
E R Y H L B U T Y Y J X O A A I T Y D F U F R F
E N C O R E S P R E J U D I C E D E G G A F S V
S V C E F O S L I H L M L O H I V N M O Q A F D
L T A H D L U S P O I L N F S C I I A I N G M Y
S S E D A B O D A R U F O P R L N R S C L E V T
T O L A E N Y L A P O S O C B O Y A T N S B S C
J B L R L A T B L U H S E R U M C I T M E I U G
C W T E L T L M N E I R A C R T F K E S N P N S
H H D Y M E H D E T D W E C N I I R S O V O X R
S T A V I N G I I N Y E O N E E I O I U I D E C
Z W A L H N M O E U T A C D O S I T N T L V Z D
F D V L I P N E Q S X M W N M L I N C B L T E W
T W W D U A P O L I T X O L E L O E E I R K R K
V C D D D G L A N O Q E C U O M R G S V C A C Y
W A E D Y I U G L R D O D B R R M K Y A N I S H
W N L P L T S B H L L E A I U N C O S W R O Q H
T E S O C T H M R L E Z U S O I F N C R M C C R
D A S I W Z X D A N L T N M U U A U E J Y Q F Q
R R V J W T Z R X L L I G Q G R S D L X S H R B
```

ABOLITIONIST	DISMAL	MESMERISM	STANCHION
ABREAST	DISPOSITION	MOURNFUL	STAVING
ADDLED	ENCHANTMENT	PALLET	STEALTHIEST
ADMIRABLE	ENCORES	PENSIVE	SUBLIME
BERTH	EVADE	PHRENOLOGY	SULTRY
BRASH	FAGGED	PIOUS	TEDIOUS
BYGONES	FEUD	PREJUDICED	VICTUALS
CANDID	FROCKS	QUICKSILVER	WADDING
COAXING	HAIL	RANSACKED	WARBLING
COLLAR	HUFFY	RASPY	WAYLAY
COMMENCED	IMPUDENT	SANCTIFIED	YAWL
CONFOUND	INSURRECTION	SHROUD	
CONVENIENCES	LATH	SOLEMN	
DERRICK	LOLLED	SOLILOQUY	

KEY: VOCABULARY WORD SEARCH - *Huckleberry Finn*

All words in this list are associated with *Huckleberry Finn* with an emphasis on the vocabulary words chosen for study in the text. The words are placed backwards, forward, diagonally, up and down. The included words are listed below.

```
            S     A D       N     D H B     H
      E   H L B U   Y     O A A I   Y     U
      E N C O R E S P R E J U D I C E D E G G A F S
      S V C E F O S   I   L M L O H I V N M O   A F
        T A H   L U S   O I L N F S C I I A I N   M Y
      S S E D A B O D A R U F O P R L N   S C L E   T
      T O   A E N Y L A P O S O C B O   A T N S B S
        L R L A T B L U H S E R U   C I T M E I U
          T E L T L M N E I R A C   T F K E S N P N S
      H H   Y M E H D E T D W E C N I I R S O   O   R
      S T A V I N G I I N Y E O N E E I O I U I   E
        W A   N M O E U T A C D O S I T N T L V   D
          L I P N E Q S X M W N M L I N C B L T E
            D U A P O L I T   O L E L O E E I R K R K
          D D D   L A N O   E C U O M R G S V C A C Y
          A E D Y I U G L   D O D B R R M K Y A N I S
          W N L P L T S     L L E A I U N C O S   R O   H
          T E S O C   M   L E   U S O I F N C R     C
          D A S I     A     T N M U U A U E
          R   V       R   L   I Q   R S D L
```

ABOLITIONIST	DISMAL	MESMERISM	STANCHION
ABREAST	DISPOSITION	MOURNFUL	STAVING
ADDLED	ENCHANTMENT	PALLET	STEALTHIEST
ADMIRABLE	ENCORES	PENSIVE	SUBLIME
BERTH	EVADE	PHRENOLOGY	SULTRY
BRASH	FAGGED	PIOUS	TEDIOUS
BYGONES	FEUD	PREJUDICED	VICTUALS
CANDID	FROCKS	QUICKSILVER	WADDING
COAXING	HAIL	RANSACKED	WARBLING
COLLAR	HUFFY	RASPY	WAYLAY
COMMENCED	IMPUDENT	SANCTIFIED	YAWL
CONFOUND	INSURRECTION	SHROUD	
CONVENIENCES	LATH	SOLEMN	
DERRICK	LOLLED	SOLILOQUY	

VOCABULARY CROSSWORD - Huckleberry Finn

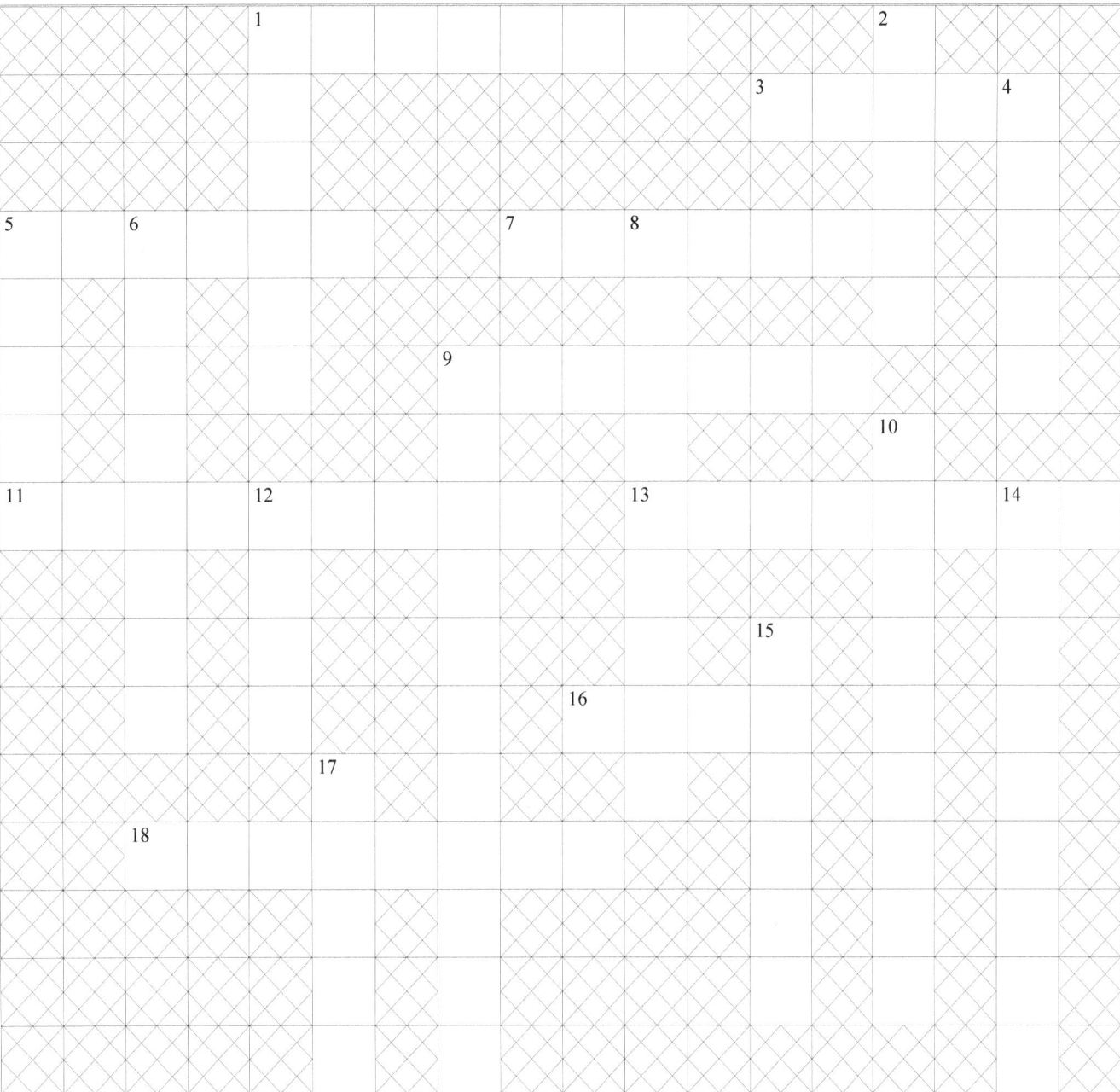

Across
1. Putting off; delaying
3. Place to sleep
5. Bunch
7. Tiresome by reason of length; boring
9. Obtaining by persistent persuasion
11. Dramatic monologue
13. Faint; feeble; sickly
16. A hereditary fight
18. Sad

Down
1. Having a respectful calm
2. Uninhibited; tactless; impudent
4. Fit of anger or annoyance
5. Religious; reverent
6. Acting with quiet caution
8. Kind of hymn
9. Fake; not real
10. Rooting through as if searching
12. Building materials
14. Post of timber or iron for support
15. Confused
17. Woman's dress

KEY: VOCABULARY CROSSWORD - Huckleberry Finn

				¹S	T	A	V	I	N	G			²B		
				O								³B	E	R	T	⁴H
				L									A		U
⁵P	⁶A	S	S	E	L		⁷T	⁸D	I	O	U	S			F
I	S							O				H			F
O	T		M			⁹C	O	A	X	I	N	G			Y
U	E		N			O		O				¹⁰R		
¹¹S	O	L	¹²I	L	O	Q	U	Y		¹³L	A	N	G	U	¹⁴I	S	H
	T		A			N				O					M		T
	H		T			T				J		¹⁵A			M		A
	Y		H			E			¹⁶F	E	U	D			A		N
			¹⁷F	R						R		D			G		C
		¹⁸M	O	U	R	N	F	U	L			L			I		H
			O			E						E			N		I
			C			I						D			G		O
			K			T											N

Across
1. Putting off; delaying
3. Place to sleep
5. Bunch
7. Tiresome by reason of length; boring
9. Obtaining by persistent persuasion
11. Dramatic monologue
13. Faint; feeble; sickly
16. A hereditary fight
18. Sad

Down
1. Having a respectful calm
2. Uninhibited; tactless; impudent
4. Fit of anger or annoyance
5. Religious; reverent
6. Acting with quiet caution
8. Kind of hymn
9. Fake; not real
10. Rooting through as if searching
12. Building materials
14. Post of timber or iron for support
15. Confused
17. Woman's dress

VOCABULARY WORKSHEET 1 - *Huckleberry Finn*

___ 1. pulled in conflicting emotional directions
  A. Staving   B. Petrified   C. Soliloquy   D. Distracted
___ 2. cloth used to wrap a body for burial
  A. Yawl   B. Berth   C. Shroud   D. Collar
___ 3. excellent; having a sense of grandeur
  A. Raspy   B. Sublime   C. Yawl   D. Passel
___ 4. past happenings
  A. Bygones   B. Distinctions   C. Temperance   D. Encores
___ 5. thoughtful
  A. Stealthy   B. Pensive   C. Petrified   D. Passel
___ 6. turned to stone
  A. Petrified   B. Pallet   C. Speculated   D. Afflicted
___ 7. to call to
  A. Frock   B. Hail   C. Ransom   D. Yawl
___ 8. person against slavery
  A. Ransomed   B. Phrenologist   C. Abolitionist   D. Impudent
___ 9. mercury
  A. Quicksilver   B. Raspy   C. Lath   D. Encore
___10. to escape or avoid by cleverness or deceit
  A. Lath   B. Evade   C. Rummaging   D. Stealthy
___11. freed from captivity for a price
  A. Candid   B. Ransomed   C. Confounded   D. Palavering
___12. differentiations
  A. Coaxing   B. Distinctions   C. Petrified   D. Sublime
___13. a woman's dress
  A. Frock   B. Afflicted   C. Yawl   D. Phrenology
___14. inclination
  A. Phrenology   B. Disposition   C. Temperance   D. Amputate
___15. to seize or detain
  A. Stanchion   B. Hail   C. Distinctions   D. Collar
___16. very humid and hot
  A. Sublime   B. Yawl   C. Sultry   D. Warbling
___17. searching
  A. Warbling   B. Rummaging   C. Coaxing   D. Petrified
___18. to cause to become confused or perplexed
  A. Collar   B. Confound   C. Commence   D. Petrify
___19. reading a person's future by examining their skull
  A. Afflict   B. Phrenology   C. Temperance   D. Petrify

KEY: VOCABULARY WORKSHEET 1 - *Huckleberry Finn*

D 1. pulled in conflicting emotional directions
    A. Staving   B. Petrified   C. Soliloquy   D. Distracted

C 2. cloth used to wrap a body for burial
    A. Yawl   B. Berth   C. Shroud   D. Collar

B 3. excellent; having a sense of grandeur
    A. Raspy   B. Sublime   C. Yawl   D. Passel

A 4. past happenings
    A. Bygones   B. Distinctions   C. Temperance   D. Encores

B 5. thoughtful
    A. Stealthy   B. Pensive   C. Petrified   D. Passel

A 6. turned to stone
    A. Petrified   B. Pallet   C. Speculated   D. Afflicted

B 7. to call to
    A. Frock   B. Hail   C. Ransom   D. Yawl

C 8. person against slavery
    A. Ransomed   B. Phrenologist   C. Abolitionist   D. Impudent

A 9. mercury
    A. Quicksilver   B. Raspy   C. Lath   D. Encore

B 10. to escape or avoid by cleverness or deceit
    A. Lath   B. Evade   C. Rummaging   D. Stealthy

B 11. freed from captivity for a price
    A. Candid   B. Ransomed   C. Confounded   D. Palavering

B 12. differentiations
    A. Coaxing   B. Distinctions   C. Petrified   D. Sublime

A 13. a woman's dress
    A. Frock   B. Afflicted   C. Yawl   D. Phrenology

B 14. inclination
    A. Phrenology   B. Disposition   C. Temperance   D. Amputate

D 15. to seize or detain
    A. Stanchion   B. Hail   C. Distinctions   D. Collar

C 16. very humid and hot
    A. Sublime   B. Yawl   C. Sultry   D. Warbling

B 17. searching
    A. Warbling   B. Rummaging   C. Coaxing   D. Petrified

B 18. to cause to become confused or perplexed
    A. Collar   B. Confound   C. Commence   D. Petrify

B 19. reading a person's future by examining their skull
    A. Afflict   B. Phrenology   C. Temperance   D. Petrify

VOCABULARY WORKSHEET 2 - *Huckleberry Finn*

___ 1. ABREAST   A. to obtain by persistent persuasion

___ 2. ADMIRABLE   B. a woman's dress

___ 3. SULTRY   C. hypnotism

___ 4. BYGONES   D. tiresome by reason of length; boring

___ 5. MESMERISM   E. to cut off

___ 6. HUFFY   F. very humid and hot

___ 7. VICTUALS   G. a preconceived preference

___ 8. BERTH   H. a hereditary fight

___ 9. SANCTIFIED   I. gloom, depression

___10. RASPY   J. a place to sleep

___11. LOLLED   K. make a risky financial transaction

___12. AMPUTATE   L. holy; inviolable

___13. TEDIOUS   M. food

___14. FROCK   N. a fit of anger or annoyance

___15. PREJUDICED   O. past happenings

___16. FEUD   P. relaxed

___17. SPECULATE   Q. grieving

___18. DISMAL   R. deserving admiration

___19. LAMENTED   S. side by side

___20. COAXING   T. grating, harsh

KEY: VOCABULARY WORKSHEET 2 - *Huckleberry Finn*

S 1. ABREAST   A. to obtain by persistent persuasion

R 2. ADMIRABLE   B. a woman's dress

F 3. SULTRY   C. hypnotism

O 4. BYGONES   D. tiresome by reason of length; boring

C 5. MESMERISM   E. to cut off

N 6. HUFFY   F. very humid and hot

M 7. VICTUALS   G. a preconceived preference

J 8. BERTH   H. a hereditary fight

L 9. SANCTIFIED   I. gloom, depression

T 10. RASPY   J. a place to sleep

P 11. LOLLED   K. make a risky financial transaction

E 12. AMPUTATE   L. holy; inviolable

D 13. TEDIOUS   M. food

B 14. FROCK   N. a fit of anger or annoyance

G 15. PREJUDICED   O. past happenings

H 16. FEUD   P. relaxed

K 17. SPECULATE   Q. grieving

I 18. DISMAL   R. deserving admiration

Q 19. LAMENTED   S. side by side

A 20. COAXING   T. grating, harsh

VOCABULARY JUGGLE LETTER REVIEW GAME CLUES - *Huckleberry Finn*

SCRAMBLED	WORD	CLUE
TITBOIANOILS	ABOLITIONIST	person against slavery
BLEISUM	SUBLIME	excellent, having a sense of grandeur
IANHNOSCT	STANCHION	post of timber or iron for support
LCEATSEPU	SPECULATE	make a risky financial transaction
ASIVCUTL	VICTUALS	food
FTIEDPERI	PETRIFIED	turned to stone
TUCONINRSREI	INSURRECTION	the act or an instance of open revolt
NDTIPUME	IMPUDENT	characterized by offensive boldness
DALEDD	ADDLED	confused
TDEAMNEL	LAMENTED	grieving
ANIGRLBW	WARBLING	singing
NBOESYG	BYGONES	past happenings
ESEMRSMIM	MESMERISM	hypnotism
ORHDSU	SHROUD	cloth used to wrap a body for burial
AGINTVRCO	CAVORTING	extravagant behavior
YFUHF	HUFFY	a fit of anger or annoyance
LNOMUUFR	MOURNFUL	sad
CSTFDIEIAN	SANCTIFIED	holy; inviolable
NAGIURMGM	RUMMAGING	searching
UTRLYS	SULTRY	very humid and hot
EUDF	FEUD	a hereditary fight
SFCROK	FROCKS	a woman's dress
AEDEV	EVADE	to escape or avoid by cleverness or deceit
MEAPAUTT	AMPUTATE	to cut off
ALLROC	COLLAR	to seize or detain
EFADGG	FAGGED	exhausted
DNCADI	CANDID	characterized by openness
LYAYWA	WAYLAY	to lie in wait for and attack from ambush
HBRAS	BRASH	uninhibited; tactless, impudent
ARDBMEAIL	ADMIRABLE	deserving admiration
DNIDAGW	WADDING	material for stopping charge in a gun
NDSKCRAAE	RANSACKED	search thoroughly or hastily
UFEISATCL	FACULTIES	any of the power or capacities possessed by the human mind
ANTTMHECNNE	ENCHANTMENT	magic; Sorcery
NONCFDOU	CONFOUND	to cause to become confused or perplexed
LEGRONOYPH	PHRENOLOGY	reading a person's future by examining their skull
YSTHTLEA	STEALTHY	marked by or acting with quiet, caution
WLYA	YAWL	small boat
ARETABS	ABREAST	side by side